T0123758

Created *for* Understanding

The Longing to Be Understood and
Understanding God and Others

Robert B. Shaw, Jr.

WESTBOW
P R E S S®
A DIVISION OF THOMAS NELSON
& ZONDERVAN

All personal anecdotes are true, but the names have changed to ensure confidentiality.

All scripture references quoted come from the New American Standard Bible, Holman Bible Publishers, Nashville, Tennessee, unless otherwise noted.

WestBow Press books may be ordered through booksellers or by contacting:

WestBow Press
A Division of Thomas Nelson & Zondervan
1663 Liberty Drive
Bloomington, IN 47403
www.westbowpress.com
844-714-3454

ISBN: 978-1-5127-5250-2 (sc)
ISBN: 978-1-5127-5251-9 (hc)
ISBN: 978-1-5127-5249-6 (e)

Library of Congress Control Number: 2016912865

Print information available on the last page.

WestBow Press rev. date: 05/22/2024

Contents

Foreword

It has often been said, that we were created *in* relationship, *through* relationship, and *for* relationship, both with God and our fellow travelers in this life. As such, we all long to better understand our Creator and to be understood by others in a deeper and more meaningful way. Commenting on His own handiwork, God said, "It is not good for the man to be alone" (Gen. 2:18). Indeed, one of His names is Emanuel, which means, "God with us" (Matt. 1:23).

Yet, the fall of man changed everything. When God asked Adam where he was, Adam replied, "I heard the sound of Thee in the garden, and I was afraid because I was naked; so I hid myself." (Gen. 3:10). From that fateful moment, whenever we are aware of our own nakedness—not in the literal sense—but when we feel the sting of rejection, or the guilt of poor choices, our natural tendency is to run and hide out of fear and shame.

Fear is a powerful motivator… and a powerful deterrent to the process of understanding. Here is my definition of fear: fear is the darkroom that develops all my negatives. Now if you're a millennial reading this, you may wonder what a "negative" is; however, for my generation, the metaphor may have a more immediate impact. Fear causes the negative things in my life to develop and at times, takeover. There is only one thing I know of that will stop a developing photograph in its tracks… light! Light has the capacity to penetrate and illuminate, while darkness cannot. When we allow the light of God's Word, His truth, His principles, and His grace shine in, the negative things that grow in the shadows simply dissipate. This book is full of light and each chapter helps unfold and reveal God's plan and design for many of the core longings within the human soul.

In the Gospel of John, Jesus said, "I am the good shepherd, and I know My own and My own know Me" (10:14). The Greek word for "know" in this verse is *ginosko*, which means to know or understand *something*. In other words, Jesus is indicating He understands His sheep and that we can also understand Him. By way of contrast, in His discourse with the young prophet, Jeremiah, God states, "Before I formed you in the womb I *knew* you…" (Jer. 1:5). In this passage, the Hebrew word for "know" is *yada* and it means to know *someone* personally, relationally, and intimately, versus only having knowledge *about* someone or something. That God could have a relationship with Jeremiah before he was even conceived is an amazing thought.

As Dr. Shaw points out, effective communication is a key factor in understanding and being understood, to have discernment and judgment, and to experience true freedom in our relationship with God. Unfortunately, some of us, perhaps too many of us, grew up with dysfunctional family rules that hindered the development of mutual understanding. Here are brief descriptions:

Rule #1 – Don't Talk – Those who grew up with this rule were not allowed to talk about anything significant or personal, especially in a transparent way. True understanding is shielded. Let's take, for example, an alcoholic father. Everyone knows dad is drinking. Everyone knows that dad comes home drunk and sometimes gets physical with mom or the kids, but no one talks about the drinking.

It's like having the proverbial elephant in the living room. We all see it. We all smell it and we see what it's doing to the carpet, but we are all supposed to tip-toe around as if it was not there. And a big "no-no"... we never tell anyone outside of the family. That would be considered treasonous. This often produces an unhealthy fear of transparency and the keeping of secrets, which can create enormous conflicts within any relationship.

Rule #2 – Don't Feel – Those who grew up with this rule were not allowed to express their feelings in an authentic way. Whenever they tried, the process would be shut down. Feelings were ignored, minimized, criticized or disallowed. Sooner or later, we come to believe that no one really cares how we are really doing, so we hide behind the hurt or the perceived threat of rejection and indifference. Again, this is an extremely destructive pattern that negatively impacts the development of intimacy and understanding in our relationships.

Rule #3 – Don't Touch – I have spoken with some adults who will tell me that as children, they have no memory of being hugged or told they were loved by the significant role models in their lives. They may have assumed it at some level, but the questions still persisted. Another possibility is that the touch was unhealthy or abusive. National statistics indicate that as many as one out of every three girls and one out of every five boys will experience some form of abuse before they graduate from high school. When I grew up, there was a saying that went like this, "Sticks and stones will break my bones, but words will never hurt me." I disagree. Long after the words are spoken or the rejection has been experienced, the emotional bruises will linger, possibly creating an unhealthy perception of intimacy. During Jesus' ministry, whenever He dealt with the demonic, more often than not, He spoke a word. However, when He healed people, He usually touched them. Appropriate physical, emotional, relational and spiritual touch are critical to healthy development and understanding.

Rule #4 – Don't Resolve – Those who grew up with this rule came to believe that nothing was resolvable or even allowed to be brought to closure. Emotional wounds were "picked at" again and again much like a scab, until a long-lasting or permanent scar was the end result. This can also translate into how believers may approach forgiveness and letting go of past hurts. They may wrestle with either receiving or giving forgiveness. Some are convinced there is no reason in trying to address and solve problems because it cannot or will not change the outcome.

Rule #5 – Don't Trust – This last rule is based, in part, on the first four. If there is no permission to talk openly, if there is no genuine expression of feelings, if there are no healthy forms of touch, and if there is no ability to bring something to successful resolution, then the hurtful conclusion is that no one can really be trusted either… even God! Being too afraid to trust leads to an independent spirit; being too hurt to love leads to pride; and being too angry to listen, leads to rebellion. Honesty and trust, especially within a Christ like environment, are like a glue that helps hold a relationship together.

This book, *Created for Understanding*, offers helpful solutions to these distorted rules of living. Readers will be treated to a compelling discussion regarding the power of communication, connection, and, relationship. Dr. Shaw draws on a wealth of practical and professional experience and provides wonderful insights, examples, and "Ah ha" moments of what it means to know and to be fully known. I highly recommend this book to all who desire deeper and more vibrant relationships. May you experience joy in the journey.

Eric Scalise, Ph.D.

President, LIV Enterprises & Consulting, LLC

Licensed Professional Counselor (LPC), and Licensed Marriage & Family Therapist (LMFT)

Past, Clinical Director, and Vice President of Professional Development at AACC

Past, Department Chair of Counseling Programs at Regent University in Virginia Beach, VA.

Introduction

One of the more frustrating experiences we can have is when we feel we have been misunderstood. All relationships (work, casual, personal, intimate, etc.) require levels of understanding for them to be fruitful, fulfilling, and satisfying. All relationships require communication. We all communicate. We all have stories. We all express ourselves. We all have messages we convey. However, we are not all understood -- at least not as often as we would like. This truth is especially pertinent in our current day and age. Fast-moving lifestyles, constant exposure to media, and changes occurring at break-neck speeds all seem to leave the ability to watch, look, and listen to one another more challenging than ever before. As discussed in my previous book, *Created for Purpose*, the devil's weapon of deception is especially effective as it relates to the ability to understand. Distractions can easily cause misunderstanding, as well.

In our day and age, we have access to a great deal of knowledge, all seemingly at our fingertips. The information highway is vast and fast, and there is the potential for information overload. As a result, we have learned to tune out many things that can often impede our ability to actually understand what we are receiving. Having a great deal of knowledge does not always translate into the ability to truly understand. Often, knowledge simply gets regurgitated back into the system, with little or no understanding of what that knowledge really conveys. Yet knowing about something or someone is not the same as understanding it or understanding them. As a result, misunderstanding occurs, and it can be frustrating and hurtful.

In addition, knowledge is not the same as wisdom. Essentially, knowledge comes from learning information. Wisdom comes from putting knowledge into action (or choosing not to) and learning by the resulting experience. Knowledge can contribute to wisdom, but wisdom is absolutely incomplete without understanding. Our decisions today are often based upon the knowledge we receive, which is indeed important. But the amount and speed of knowledge that comes our way is often like drinking from a fire hose. If we would spend the time and slow down the process, become more aware of our surroundings and the people around us, and take note of what is *really* occurring in our time, we would have a better chance of developing understanding and wisdom, whereby better decisions can be made.

Everything is too fast today, including our decision making. Understanding needs contemplation, and contemplation takes time. Everyone's life would benefit much more if we would simply take the time to consider and contemplate what we take in before we think and act. While most people believe they do so, I have found that this is not the case. We have become so used to the speed of life, that we have become desensitized to the process of understanding and using wisdom.

To be understood is a human core longing. We all want people to truly understand us, our messages, our hearts, and our intentions. Core longings are meant to draw us ultimately into God's embrace, to find rest, and to experience true contentment. This is the fourth book in the series of six dealing with core longings. I want to acknowledge Dr. Terry Wardle and Dr. Anne Halley for their teaching on human longings and on inner healing prayer. In this series we have been identifying and exploring the aspects and fulfillment of each of the core longings:

- significance
- safety (covering)
- purpose
- *understanding*
- belonging
- love

In order for us to be truly understood, certain truths need to exist, and we will discuss them in the pages set before you. You will learn what it means to be understood and why it is important; several areas of misunderstanding that I believe are common; the role of conviction in the process of understanding; and how to rein in the truth when needed to help understanding take place.

To understand something or someone is having the knowledge, and then applying that knowledge, to gain reality and wisdom. Also, to discern the intentions of someone brings understanding of his or her words and behavior. First, we need to understand God, although for us to completely understand Him would no longer render Him God. The first few chapters will discuss some common aspects that could help better understand God and His kingdom. I realize countless volumes have been written throughout human history that are much more thorough with that goal in mind, and so the following pages are nutshell attempts to assist in understanding God –- and I do so ever so humbly. Ultimately, after all that we read and do, faith and trust in God are essential.

Second, we need to understand ourselves and others, which is a much more achievable endeavor. We have not been created to live on an isolated island, so therefore, the ability to understand one another aids in the closeness needed for satisfying relationships. To feel at ease with someone and to be understood is a great feeling. Realizing that another person knows your heart and even your tendencies, and yet accepts you, is an experience that is hard to match.

We all have the longing to be understood. We want others to understand us. For another person to understand us they would need to know our thoughts, tendencies, intentions, feelings, desires, and personality, just to name a few. Someone also needs to listen, not just hear, when someone else speaks. Parents raise their children and as time moves forward, they learn their children's personalities, tendencies, and desires. Equipped with such understanding, parents can then help guide their children towards their destiny. One important goal in a marriage is for each spouse to understand, or know each other. When understanding occurs, relational aspects such as communication in marriage, the meeting of each other's needs, and sexual fulfillment, are enhanced.

The Bible makes it clear that God truly understands us. In the beginning, God created human beings in His own image. As a result, the Lord knows everything and understands everything about men and women. We have been intricately created. Psalms 139:13--16 states:

> For you formed my inward parts; You wove me in my mother's womb. I will give thanks to You, for I am fearfully and wonderfully made; wonderful are Your works, and my soul knows it very well. My frame was not hidden from You, when I was made in secret, and skillfully wrought in the depths of the earth; Your eyes have seen my unformed substance; and in Your book were all written the days that were ordained for me, when as yet there was not one of them.

God understands the human body and soul and the life that we live on earth. He truly sees us accurately and in truth. He knows our inner desires and His plan for each individual. Jesus also experienced grief, betrayal, abuse, rejection, scorn, false accusations, misunderstanding, and demanding expectations. He surely knows our plights in life.

My prayer is that as you gain the understanding needed in the many areas of your day-to-day life, you will grow in discernment of God, yourself, and the people around you. Also, I pray that you can understand yourself better as you read this book and have others understand you better as well. Ultimately, your relationships will then become more satisfying and your life will have a new level of wisdom, peace, and contentment.

PART I
Understanding God

CHAPTER 1

Communication –- The Essence of Understanding

> God, after He spoke long ago to the fathers in the prophets in many portions and in many ways, in these last days has spoken to us in His Son.
>
> –- Hebrews 1:1–-2

> If you had known Me, you would have known My Father also; from now on you know Him, and have seen Him. . . . He who has seen Me has seen the Father.
>
> –- John 13:7–-9

> I and the Father are One.
>
> –- John 10:30

As a child, I remember playing a game that would reveal to us the challenges of communication. Because of technology, I do not get the impression that it is played much anymore, although I have recently heard that some teachers play this game as a fun way to educate their young students. The game would consist of a large group, usually more than twenty people, seated in a circle, and with everyone facing each other. One person would begin with a statement, whispering it in the ear of the person to his or her left or right.

Then, that person would likewise whisper the same statement, as he or she heard it, to the person seated next to them, and so on. This would continue until the message was received by the last person seated in the circle. The last person would then declare the statement to everyone, as he or she heard it. Almost always, the declared message at the end of the game was different from what it was when it was first whispered at the beginning of the circle. The lesson of this game was to see the importance of communication, listening, and understanding the message.

Another common game that was played by both young people and adults is pantomime or charades. A person acts out the name of a person, place, or thing using only body language and hand motions. The rest of the group playing the game has the challenge of guessing the name while the actor provides no sound. Often the name of a person, place, or thing has to be broken up into segments that are then combined to determine the hidden meaning and identity. It is amazing to watch how something can be communicated and understood without a word. As we will see, non-verbal communication is just as, if not more, effective.

Communication is an essential aspect in any relationship. It is important in business transactions. When a contract is created, the wording is important. The parties involved in the business transaction want to know clearly the arrangements are to which they are agreeing. Often the fine print is designed to provide statements that are not always read, and as a result, misunderstanding can occur and conflict between the parties can develop.

When I purchased a minivan years ago for my family, I was given a warranty agreement. The warranty agreement stated the many things about the vehicle that were covered should something go wrong. Sometimes the sales person briefly reviews what is covered under the warranty, but there are always stipulations and fine print not discussed. Most of us do not take the time to read the warranty document, and I was certainly guilty of that as well. One day, the rear windshield wiper stopped working, and I took it to the dealer to redeem the warranty. They discovered that the motor had burned out and needed replacing. They also assured me that it was covered under the warranty.

Later in the day, the dealer called to inform me that the burned-out motor was not covered after all. I re-read the warranty, and it said that the windshield wiper motors were indeed covered. The dealer too was under that assumption until they called the company's home office. The home office informed them that the "windshield" only referred to the front glass. The rear glass is not called the "windshield" but rather the "rear window," and therefore the rear wiper was not covered under the warranty. Needless to say, I was quite miffed by this understanding of the warranty. The dealer was even frustrated with the explanation. I learned it is important to be sure that the same understanding of certain terms is shared by the parties involved.

Understanding in communication is necessary in sports when playing together as a team. In football, the terminology for each play needs to be understood by all the players. Otherwise not everyone on the team will execute the same play. In baseball, when a catcher calls for a certain pitch using finger signs, it is important that the pitcher knows the signs for each pitch. If not, the pitcher will throw the wrong pitch, and the team may experience anything from a stolen base to a homerun. Understanding the rules for any sport and any game is essential for the participants to play by the rules, or else they might experience unwanted consequences as a result.

It is critical in the military for communication to be understood, especially in the midst of combat operations. Hand signals, strategies, and even the understanding of the use of certain weapons and equipment can be a matter of life or death. The term *friendly fire* was coined to describe a fire fight between members of the same army, when both sides believed they were engaging with the enemy. Such a potentially deadly situation is a result of miscommunication or misunderstanding.

Communication can make or break a marriage relationship. At one time, the top three reasons why couples came to counseling were financial issues, in-law issues, and sexual issues. In my experience they are now two, three, and four on the list. The top reason for conflict by far is communication issues. Of course, generally speaking, communication has a lot to do with financial decisions, sexual intimacy, and relationships with the in-laws, but a lack of basic communication and understanding is unfortunately rampant today.

Misinterpreting a person's motives or intentions is a common barrier contributing to the lack of understanding someone. We all have filters through which we speak and through which we listen that often hinder understanding. Some of the most common hindering filters are assumptions, personal agendas, self-centeredness, and bitterness caused by hurt and unforgiveness. Many of these filters will be discussed in subsequent chapters.

Ultimately, communication is needed in our relationship with God. Many of us complain that we do not hear God; that we do not understand God; that we do not understand His Word; or that we do not understand what He wants from us. I discuss some of these aspects in my previous book, *Created for Purpose*. What we tend to overlook is that God is constantly speaking to us. He is not relegated to speaking only through the conventional way that we all are used to –- mouth to ears.

As Creator, He creatively speaks through His Word, creation, circumstances, dreams, symbols, and signs and wonders, just to name a few. While science can be utilized to reveal and understand God and His order in the universe, many scientists have instead used science to diminish God. Discussing unbelievers and those who suppress the truth, the apostle Paul writes in Romans 1:20:

> That is which is known about God is evident within them; for God made it evident to them. For since the creation of the world His invisible attributes, His eternal power and divine nature, have been clearly seen, being understood through what has been made, so that they are without excuse.

The same filters that hinder communication between each other prevent us from hearing from God as well. Unbelief, personal agendas, emotional pain, assumptions, resentment, and simply a lack of communication (prayer) can prevent true understanding and knowledge of the truth.

Components of Communication

There are three components of communication. The first component is *content* –- which is *what* is being said. The content of our communication is often what we emphasize and on which we focus. The reality is, however, that content is only *7 percent* of communication. In today's world of electronic devices and the Internet, the only thing that is communicated is content. And while we are the most "connected" generation ever in human history, we still have problems understanding each other. Electronic grammar, spelling, etc., often impede what is being said. For example, we have texting, blogging, tweeting, hangouts, emails, Facebook, and LinkedIn, yet we are frustrated with a lack of understanding that we feel from one another. This is because we focus on just the content of communication –– only 7 percent of what is being conveyed.

The second component of communication is *tone of voice* –– which is *how* it is being said. Inflection, volume, and pitch are aspects of tone of voice. Tone of voice is *38 percent* of communication. When someone is speaking too softly, what can be communicated is that he or she is afraid, too shy, not confident, apathetic, soft-spoken, or fatigued just to name a few. How we say something conveys a meaning that will often affect the content's meaning, which can frustrate the "transmitter" who may feel misunderstood. It can also frustrate the receiver, because they did not understand the transmitter.

On the other hand, if someone is yelling, the content may be ignored and the feeling of being hurt, demeaned, or overwhelmed often drowns out the content. We focus on how we *felt* over what we *heard* because of tone of voice.

The third component of communication is *non-verbal* –– which is *body language*, *gestures*, and the use of *objects*. This aspect is often overlooked, yet it comprises *55 percent* of communication! Body language –– like walking away from a conversation, rolling of the eyes, folding of the arms over our chests, facial expressions, and hand gestures –– are just some ways communication is presented. Such body language will express something that will either enhance the content of our communication or detract from it. Misunderstanding will often occur because of what we exhibit in our body language.

For example, if a husband is on his smart phone reading his emails, or if he is watching television while his wife is trying to speak to him, the wife will often get frustrated and feel as if he is not interested or is ignoring her. She may feel unimportant. If she were to explain her feelings, the husband may be at a loss as to why she is so upset. He may say something like, "But I was listening" or "But I did not say a word" or "What did I do?" or "Don't be ridiculous." He may have had no idea that his non-verbal communication conveyed to his wife that he was not engaged in the conversation, not to mention being rude. Instead, if he shut off the television, for example, and made eye contact with his wife, his body language would have communicated something totally different –– that he cared and that he was interested in what she had to say.

The core longing to be understood hinges upon our ability to properly communicate and feel connected. We may be highly connected through media, but we have become terrible communicators. Unless someone is Skyping, the majority of communication is being missed through media communication. Even Skyping can leave a lot to be desired. Again, we have become focused on content through media connections, but there is so much more to communication. As a result, we are misunderstood.

People today generally have a difficult time learning the skills of good communication, despite the many ways of electronic communication in our day and age. Just think how often you are frustrated with automated customer service numbers. It would be nice to be able to speak to a live and breathing person, who understands our language, to have our concerns met, right? Good communication skills are not found through media vehicles. We may be the most "connected" global society that ever existed, but ironically, we have fewer communication skills than ever before. For example,

- 92 percent of all Americans own a cell phone

- 42 percent of American adults own a tablet computer
- 63 percent use their phones to access the Internet
- 79 percent send and receive texts
- Those ages eighteen to twenty-four send an average of 110 texts per day
- Twenty-one million Americans use twitter at least once per month
- There are thirty-one million American bloggers
- 74 percent of online adults use Facebook
- 56 percent of all Americans have a profile, and
- 22 percent of online adults use LinkedIn (Pew Research Center online, 2014)

Good communication, and the ability to understand each other, is still found in interpersonal interaction between flesh and blood. Our high-tech preferences cannot replace the high touch factors of good communication.

Communication becomes an issue when we feel that our core longing of being understood is not taking place. It is discouraging, hurtful, and frustrating. Being misunderstood or even overlooked can lead to depression, anger, and self-esteem issues, to name a few. We often want to be alone as a result of constant misunderstanding. On the other hand, it could lead to broken relationships. Many affairs begin because we feel connected to someone who is willing to listen and understand us. Yet, God created us to be in relationships. So, there is a conflict within us when we feel like no one really knows us, and yet we desire to be known by someone.

In the 2009 movie *Avatar*, distributed by 20th Century Fox, there were several lines that reflected understanding between the characters. In the movie, the natives of the planet Pandora, the Na'vi people, would say, "I see you." They would utter that statement to indicate that another person was understood and that they have come to know them better than before. It communicated understanding and intimacy. This was said between the characters Neytiri and Jake Sully, especially toward the end of the movie. As Sully became more like the Na'vi people, Neytiri grew to trust him and she was able to say to him, "I see you."

To be understood, therefore, is to be seen. But not just with the eyes. In Genesis 16, God speaks to Hagar, who was wandering in the wilderness with her son, Ishmael. They were abused by Sarah, Abraham's wife, and were eventually kicked out of the household, even though it was Sarah who encouraged Abraham to have a child with Hagar. God addressed Hagar and spoke of her plight and His desire to care for her and her child. Hagar responded in verse 13: "Then she called the name of the Lord who spoke to her, 'Thou art a God who sees.'" In the Hebrew language it is even more personal. She was saying, "You God, truly do see me." We know we are seen when someone acknowledges us and sees our heart, intentions, situation, and personality, as well as our actions. It is essential, therefore, to have our actions line up with our intentions as much as possible. It is also helpful to get to know a person in order to understand his or her actions.

God knows all about communication. From the beginning of time, He has communicated to His creation and especially to humankind. All creation, except for human beings, was created by God's spoken word. Effective communication, indeed! Adam was created in a more intimate fashion. God used "body language," if you will, when he *formed* man from the dust of the ground (Gen. 2:7). Then God *breathed* into him and made him a living soul (Gen. 2:7). When God created woman, He essentially continued His intimate

11

communication with humans and took from man a rib, and *formed* a woman, and brought the woman to man (Gen. 2:21--22). Body language, indeed.

When God breathed into man, He imparted His image to us. As a result, all human beings are essentially spiritual beings, yet we often ignore this truth. John 4:24 states, "God is Spirit, and those who worship Him must worship in spirit and truth." We are essentially spirit beings as well, and we can only understand God through our spirit. God understands us, and we have capacity to understand God. At least Adam and Eve understood, before the rebellion in the Garden of Eden. Since then, we struggle to understand God, even though He completely and intimately understands us.

So God decided to communicate with men and women throughout biblical history in such a way that we could understand Him. However, the truth remains that while we are in this fallen, sinful world, *complete* understanding of God will escape us. We can, however, grow in our understanding of God through certain disciplines -- mostly by slowing down and hearing and seeing Him where He is to be found.

From the beginning, creation, symbols, and the spoken word were used to communicate about God. The stars and constellations were understood by ancient cultures as a way that God was using to convey His message to humankind (see appendix for resources about this). Ancient cultures used oral tradition and the spoken word to convey history and truths about God. The ancient peoples before Abraham used storytelling, writings, hieroglyphics, and symbols to communicate content from generation to generation. Later, the nation of Israel employed scribes to enhance oral tradition into written form, in order to preserve the truths about God and His plan for humankind. So early in biblical history *content* was communicated from God and about God, His love for us, His dealings with human beings, and His plan.

Then, as history progressed, God became disappointed and angry with Israel, who began to move away from Him. As a result, He adjusted His communication style somewhat and began to send prophets to the people to express His disappointment and anger as well as His love. If we read any of the prophets, the Major Prophets, like Ezekiel and Isaiah, and the Minor Prophets, such as Joel, Hosea, and Micah, we come away hearing a *tone of voice* in God's message. Here are a few examples:

> Wash yourselves, make yourselves clean; Remove the evil of your deeds from my sight. Cease to do evil, learn to do good; Seek justice, reprove the ruthless; Defend the orphan, plead for the widow. . . If you consent and obey, you will eat the best of the land; But if you refuse and rebel, you will be devoured by the sword." Truly the mouth of the Lord has spoken. (Isaiah 1:16–17, 19–20)

> Listen to the word of the Lord, O sons of Israel, for the Lord has a case against the inhabitants of the land, because there is no faithfulness or kindness or knowledge of God in the land. There is swearing, deception, murder, stealing, and adultery. They employ violence, so that bloodshed follows bloodshed. . . Harlotry, wine, and new wine take away the understanding. My people consult their wooden idol, and their diviner's wand informs them; For a spirit of harlotry has lead them astray, and they have played the harlot, departing from their God. (Hosea 4:1–2, 11–12)

> "Thus I will establish my covenant with you, and you shall know that I am the Lord, in order that you may remember

and be ashamed, and never open your mouth anymore because of your humiliation, when I have forgiven you for all that you have done," the Lord God declares. (Ezekiel 16:62--63)

God's tone of voice still expressed love for His people and He was angry because they had turned away from Him. Yet, in His anger, admonishment, and correction God expressed a loss of relationship with His chosen people, His desire to see them return to Him, and how He felt about their rebellion and idolatry.

God made it increasingly clear that He longed for restoration and cared enough for His people to want them to return to Him and put aside selfishness, rebellion, and unfaithfulness. His tone often caused Him to be misunderstood, as He was seen as an angry God looking to discipline His people, and at times that was true. God was responding as a Father would when He witnessed the choices made by His children that led them away from relationship with Him. God's tone conveyed a desire to have His children see their sinful choices and wayward behavior. The Father's intent was to correct, and through discipline, bring them back into relationship with Him. Correction is not rejection -- for the Word says, "For whom the Lord loves, He reproves, even as a father, the son in whom he delights" (Prov. 3:12). The content that expressed His love for people and hatred of sin and evil was misunderstood because of His expressed displeasure. God was angry about the separation caused by their activity of sin, but He still loved His people.

If we think about how our parents communicated to us their displeasure, we can remember feeling as if they did not love us, when in reality they loved so much to desire protection and better choices than maybe we were making. If we are parents, we can truly relate

14

to this and understand the feelings toward our children. Consider Hebrews 12:5--11:

> My son do not regard lightly the discipline of the Lord, nor faint when you are reproved by Him; For those whom the Lord loves He disciplines . . . for God deals with you as with sons [or daughters]; for what son is there whom his father does not discipline? But if you are without discipline, of which all have become partakers, then you are illegitimate children and not sons . . . He disciplines us for our good, that we may share His holiness. All discipline for the moment seems not to be joyful, but sorrowful; yet to those who have been trained by it, afterwards it yields the peaceful fruit of righteousness. [additions mine]

God, as our Father, communicates with those He loves, even through discipline, that He desires us to be in relationship with Him, and to guide us away from our bad choices, which usually lead to bad consequences.

Finally, God expressed His love ultimately through *body language.* For thousands of years of biblical history, God conveyed *content* where He expressed His love for us, yet it did not sustain our understanding of God. The hundreds of years of God's *tone of voice* through the prophets' messages also did not sustain true understanding of God's desire for us. Then the writer of Hebrews declares a shift in how God chose to communicate to human beings:

> God, after He spoke long ago to the fathers in the prophets in many portions and in many ways, in these last days has spoken to us *in His Son*, whom He appointed heir of all things, through whom also He made the world. And He

is the radiance of His glory and the *exact representation* of His nature, and upholds all things by the word of His power (Heb. 1:1–3) (italics mine).

So He sent Jesus –– the ultimate non-verbal, body language-type of communication from God! God showed up in the flesh –– Jesus Christ –– to help us understand who He is.

Sure, Jesus spoke a lot. However, it was also what He *did* through miracles, signs and wonders, death, and resurrection that conveyed His love for human beings through more than mere words. In referring to the Son of God, the writer of Hebrews says:

For this reason we must pay much closer attention to what we have heard, lest we drift away from it. For if the word spoken through angels proved unalterable, and every transgression and disobedience received a just recompense, how shall we escape if we neglect so great a salvation? After it was at first spoken through the Lord, it was confirmed to us by those who heard, God also bearing witness with them, both by signs and wonders and by various miracles and by gifts of the Holy Spirit according to His own will (Heb. 2:1–4).

The word *angels* means "messengers" and they were employed by God to carry both His content and sometimes His tone of voice to human beings. If what angels conveyed was steadfast truth, how much more by showing up in the flesh through Jesus's life, teaching, and miracles communicates truth? In fact, Jesus pronounced that He *is* the truth! He is our great salvation. He is God in the flesh. God is revealed through the life of Jesus. God's love, power, mercy, holiness, hatred of sin but grace for the sinner, and desire to be in our lives is seen through Jesus. Colossians 2:9 says, "For in Him all the fullness of Deity dwells in bodily form." Also, Colossians 1:19 declares, "For it was the Father's good pleasure for all the fullness to dwell in Him." Complete, ultimate body language!

Listen to content in John 1:1--5:

In the beginning was the *Word*, and the *Word* was with God, and the *Word* was God. He was in the beginning with God. All things came into being by Him, and apart from Him nothing came into being that has come into being. In Him was life, and the life was the light of men. And the light shines in the darkness, and the darkness did not *comprehend* (*understand*) it. (emphasis mine)

Then, as we read further in John's gospel, we read: "And the Word *became flesh*, and dwelt among us, and we *beheld* His glory, glory as of the only begotten from the Father, full of grace and truth" (John 1:14)(italics mine). Body language! God came in bodily form to show us His love, grace and truth. Jesus said, "I am the Way, and the truth, and the Life; no one comes to the Father, but through Me" (John 14:6). Jesus was God's body language, to show us who He is -- to underscore the content of His love; to underscore the tone of voice of His love; and to help us understand the true nature of God.

Jesus's ministry was more than spoken word. He performed miracles -- bringing the love of God and the kingdom of God to earth. He still performs miracles today because it is His nature to show forth His love and not just speak it. He was betrayed, laid down His life, and was abused and crucified on our behalf (Matt. 27:26--50). He then rose from the dead, conquering death. God's body language through Jesus communicates to us the primary key to understand Him! I believe Jesus's declaration that "no one comes to the Father, but through Me" can now make sense to all nations. We can understand God through Jesus. We can get to know God through Jesus. We can be healed through Jesus. We can be restored to a relationship with God through Jesus –- but only through Jesus. We can better understand God because of Jesus.

In Jesus, we can also declare that God knows us. Not only is it important to understand God, we need to know that God really understands us. Does He really care and see what is going on in our lives? Does God get it? The truth is He understands us. We are created in His image. We reflect Him. But does He really understand what I am going through? Can a big, seemingly distant God truly relate to the struggles, doubt, abuse, and so forth, that I have experienced in life? Well, the truth is that He can because of Jesus.

Jesus walked in our shoes and understands us. Jesus left His heavenly role as God the Son and lived a human life filled with joy and sadness; courage and fear; care and abuse; love and hatred; friendship and betrayal; being received, as well as being misunderstood; joy and despair; having demands placed upon Him; being falsely accused; and of course, life and death. "Jesus was God's visible version of 'me too' Every pain you've ever experienced or been through in your life, God can say, 'Me too' . . . you name it, Jesus understands" (Weece 2016, 6). Hebrews 4:15–-16 states:

> Since then we have a great high priest who has passed through the heavens, Jesus the Son of God, let us hold fast our confession. For we do not have a high priest who cannot sympathize with our weaknesses, but one who has been tempted in all things as we are, yet without sin. Let us therefore draw near with confidence to the throne of

grace, that we may receive mercy and may find grace to
help in time of need.

As for Christians, we are called to present Jesus to the world. The church is called the *body* of Christ (Rom. 12:4–-5) and as such we are ambassadors for the kingdom of heaven. Since Jesus ascended to heaven after His resurrection, the church has become God's body language. Jesus even declared, "Truly, truly I say to you, he who believes in Me, the works that I do shall he do also; and *greater works* than these shall he do, because I go the Father" (John 14:12; emphasis mine). The church's mission is more than just information, institution, and inspiration –- it is supposed to be about revelation and transformation! The church is to be Jesus to others. That includes showing forth love and mercy, but also holiness, correction, and restoration. It also includes miracles, signs, and wonders, but also the general kindness and care that are required during times of need. There is a balance, as there was in the life of Jesus.

Finally, when Jesus returns at the end of the age, it will not be a hidden return. He will not come back for just a few to notice. He will not come back "in spirit" only. He will return with full body language as, ". . . *every* eye will *see* Him" (Rev. 1:7, emphasis mine).

The next few chapters will present some misunderstood biblical concepts. My intent is to try to provide some basic insight into some common misunderstandings of God and His kingdom.

CHAPTER 2

Understanding the Kingdom of God

Therefore I have declared that which I did not understand, things too wonderful for me, which I did not know.

— Job 42:3

And the one on whom seed was sown on the good soil, this is the man who hears the word and understands it; who indeed bears fruit, and brings forth, some a hundredfold, some sixty, and some thirty.

— Matthew 13:23

He who gets wisdom loves his own soul; he who keeps understanding will find good.

— Proverbs 19:8

God's kingdom is an upside-down kingdom. Concepts conveyed in scripture often seem to contradict one another, thereby rendering common misunderstandings about God and His ways. As we grow in relationship with God, He reveals more of Himself

20

and we grow to understand more, even if it is by faith alone. Isaiah 55:7–9 states:

> Let the wicked forsake his way, and the unrighteous man his thoughts; And let him return to the Lord, and He will have compassion on him; And to our God, for He will abundantly pardon. "For My thoughts are not your thoughts, neither are your ways My ways," declares the Lord. "For as the heavens are higher than the earth, so are My ways higher than your ways And My thoughts than your thoughts."

This verse is simply saying that our human way of thinking does not do justice to the ways of God. Our thinking is so limited and clouded by selfishness and sin that it takes revelation and transformation by the Spirit of God in order to begin to understand God. In order to understand God, we must be willing to surrender our fallen way of thinking and ask the Lord to show us Himself. He is faithful, and I believe He desires to speak to us. I encourage you to ask God to reveal Himself to you, in whatever state and circumstances you are in, and He will do it!

We tend to want to form God in our image, when the truth is we are made in His image. While we are in the world, things seem upside down or backward compared to the kingdom of God and His ways. First, there is the understanding that we must be child-like. To be the greatest, we must be the least; to be free, we must be dependent.

Second, we must understand that our life is not our own and our true strength does not come from us. To gain we must lose; to win we must surrender; to be strong we must be weak; to overflow in power we must be empty of ourselves. To receive we must give; the first shall be last.

21

Third, it is essential to understand that what we experience in the world is not always what God values. The wisdom of God is often foolishness to the world, and the wisdom of the world is often sin and foolishness to God. There has developed confusion as to the role of the church in our world today. There is much confusion in the world and the church regarding the "unforgiveable sin." We will discuss these aspects in order to provide some understanding.

Most of the above contrasts that appear in scripture have to do with control -- who controls our life. Jesus taught, but also modeled for us, an approach to life that was one of dependency upon God. His dependency upon the Father not only produced great power, but also tremendous peace. His humility and obedience produced great exaltation and glory. His connection to the Father produced great understanding. Philippians 2:5--11 states:

> Have this attitude in yourselves which was also in Christ Jesus, who, although He existed in the form of God, did not regard equality with God a thing to be grasped, but emptied Himself, taking the form of a bond-servant, and being made in the likeness of men. And being found in appearance as a man, He humbled Himself by becoming obedient to the point of death, even death on a cross. Therefore also God highly exalted Him, and bestowed on Him the name which is above every name, that at the name of Jesus every knee should bow, of those who are in heaven and on the earth, and under the earth, and every tongue should confess that Jesus Christ is Lord, to the glory of God the Father.

Finally, there were several times when people arrived at a simple understanding of God through life-changing experiences. These experiences are samples that illustrate that we do not need to know everything about God to believe in Him and accept Him. Encounters with God have a way of dramatically altering our lives, and I believe He continues to look for ways to communicate with us through revelation. My prayer is that God will further reveal Himself to you and increase your understanding through these contrasts and stories to the degree that you will grow in freedom and devotion to Him.

Childish vs. Childlike

When my oldest daughter was in kindergarten, we had one of many special moments. She had early release one day, and she and I went to a fast food restaurant for lunch. This particular restaurant had an outdoor playground, and after ordering our food, we sat outside so she could play. After playing for a few minutes, she ran up to me, obviously upset about something.

She said, "Dad, that little boy said I was ugly!"

Once I took a few moments to collect myself from wanting to pulverize the other kid, I simply said to my daughter, "Your mom and I have always told you that you were beautiful, so what is the truth?"

Without saying a word, a smile immediately came upon her face, and she turned around and quickly skipped back to the playground, empowered by a renewed understanding of the truth. That was as meaningful and impactful to me, as it was to my daughter that day. Her understanding of the truth, and her innocent acceptance of it from her father, transformed her countenance and her confidence. She became free because she incorporated her understating of the truth. It allowed me to see how the sweet, childlike dependency upon someone who loved her was so important in restoring her understanding. Despite what other people say about us, or have done to us, our Father tells us many things such as, we are loved;

we are valued; we are cherished; and we are competent. If only we could innocently know how much our heavenly Father wants to communicate truth about His love for us, it would change our countenance and approach to life -- even in the face of hurt and lies.

Jesus taught that we needed the faith of a child to enter into His kingdom. Jesus said in Matthew 18:3--4, "Truly I say to you, unless you are converted and become like children, you shall not enter the kingdom of heaven. Whoever then humbles himself as this child, he is the greatest in the kingdom of heaven." Jesus was responding to the question, "Who is the greatest?" in the kingdom of heaven. He did not mean that we are to remain immature or childish. Rather, He was indicating that we become humble and dependent upon Him. We were not created to be independent from God, but to rely upon Him for our strength, guidance, hope, and life. (See the book, *Created for Covering*).

Later, Jesus responded to a group of children who came to Him, and the disciples wanted to send them away. He stated, "Let the children alone, and do not hinder them from coming to Me; for the kingdom of heaven belongs to such as these" (Matt. 19:14). Jesus makes it clear to adults around Him that child-likeness is not to be ignored. Children have access to God and have a voice that the Lord will listen to.

As youngsters, we have been often told, "Children are to be seen and not heard." Children who understood that they were to be seen and not heard may be among the children who felt they could not speak up and tell someone that they were being sexually or physically abused. That is part of the tragedy of abuse -- believing one has no voice. Abuse is devastating to the victim. Add to that the belief that no one will listen to the voice he or she has, and a sense of feeling powerless and alone, a victim will feel devastated. Jesus wants to hear the innocence of a child and the voice of a hurting child. He warned in Matthew 18:6, "But whoever causes one of these little ones who believe in Me to stumble, it is better for him that a heavy millstone be hung around his neck, and that he be drowned in the depth of the sea."

Children are dependent, enthusiastic, innocent, playful, and usually willing to please. These qualities, and more, are what God desires to see in someone who follows after Him. We are rendered innocent when we confess our brokenness and come to Jesus for salvation. Our willingness to please is such an important aspect of our relationship with God, that it cannot be understated. Our willingness to please should be a result of our love for Him, not because we feel we have to earn His love. Our childlikeness actually increases our ability to understand the Lord. We often become so sophisticated in our faith that our dependency upon God diminishes. After we accept Christ, adults often return to a headiness and self-dependency again. As a result, we hamper the ability to understand God and His desires for our life. Humility, dependency, and gratitude are essential in developing the understanding of God we need.

Childishness, on the other hand, leads us in the opposite direction from relationship with God. Childishness is immaturity. Immaturity is regarded as showing a lack of adult qualities such as emotional restraint, seriousness when needed, *giving* of self instead of *taking* for self, critical thinking skills, or exhibiting good sense. I am sure most of us can picture occasions in grocery stores or department stores when we witnessed a child throwing a temper tantrum. The tantrum happened because the child was demanding his or her own way or perhaps reacting to the word *no* from the parent. Unfortunately, many adults exhibit tantrums too, but they show up in more "sophisticated" ways. One of those ways is when adults push for things with the mentality, "I'll show you!" We often are not aware of such a mind-set, but it exists because of childish anger. The essential difference is childlikeness is innocently dependent, while childishness is selfishly demanding!

The spiritual fruit of self-control is in total opposition to our society's norms. We want what we want when we want it. When we don't receive what we demand, we turn against God, other people, and even societal norms. We operate under the assumption of entitlement instead of the truth that all that we have are gifts. Entitlement is a characteristic of childishness. Jesus said, "Beware, and be on your guard against every form of greed; for not even when one has an abundance does his life consist of his possessions" (Luke 12:15). Childishness wants to receive –- maturity wants to give. Childishness does not like to wait for things. Childishness does not like to hear "No!" for an answer. We are after instant gratification instead of delayed gratification. Yet the Bible teaches that the love of Christ constrains us (2 Cor. 5:14, KJV). Many times we are more loved when we do *not* receive what we ask for, than by receiving what we want. When we understand that, we are developing maturity.

God's love is such that he knows what is best and if need be, will choose to delay. God's nature is to give, so if He chooses to wait, it must be because we are not ready. An ancient Christian church father had an interesting interpretation of the forbidden tree in the Garden of Eden that perhaps may shed some light on this discussion:

> Saint Irenaeus was the bishop of Lyons a little more than 100 years after the time of Christ. He concluded that the reason Adam was forbidden to eat the fruit was not that it was bad, but instead, that he just wasn't ready. In other words, he just needed to grow up first before he had all the knowledge that the fruit could give. God was treating

him much the same way we treat our children who ask really hard questions at really young ages. We might say something like, "When you are older I'll explain that to you. You are just too young now." It is not just a matter of growing up but growing up in the right way in the right time. Unfortunately, Adam, in his impatience to grow up, disobeyed God, ate the fruit and knew too much too soon. He grew up too fast. That happens in our world far too often. Either of our own choosing or sometimes it is forced upon us, we lose our childish innocence and take on false "grown-upness." The little girl that is abused, the teenage boy that is rejected; we decide that the world is not a safe place and we'd better take care of ourselves. We force ourselves to grow up. The only way to correct our false grown-upness is to become again a little child and allow Christ to help us grow up again in the right way, loved, nurtured and supported by an incredible loving Father. Counselors might call it "discovering your inner child" (*Mastering Life*, 2008).

Our spiritual maturity is not measured by what we can do without God; rather, it is measured by what He can do through us and how much we reflect God! Our emotional maturity is measured by how much we can control our desires for self-gratification in the midst of great temptation and our current have-it-now environment. Our mental maturity is measured by whether we are able to discern the spirits of the moment and make a truth-based decision (more on this later). All efforts to walk in maturity are based upon our understanding of the truths of God as it applies to life. Understanding should empower us to respond to wisdom, and not impulses.

In what we know to be the "love chapter" in scripture, I Corinthians 13, Paul makes a statement that seems to be out of place. He writes, "When I was a child, I used to speak as a child, think as a child, reason as a child; when I became a man, I did away with childish things" (I Cor. 13:11). When one looks at the entire context of the chapter, I believe it should be called the "mature chapter," not the "love chapter," because the description of the aspects of love is for those who are indeed mature and not childish. (More on this in my book, *Created for Love*). A childish person could not possibly express love the way love is to be expressed as described in I Corinthians 13.

Losing or Giving Is to Gain vs. Finding or Keeping Is to Lose

One of the many challenges of World War II was the bombing missions the Allies had to conduct that helped win the war in both Europe and Japan. One challenge was the distance the bombers had to fly in order to hit the designated targets, and then return home safely. Often the concern was whether the planes had enough fuel or were light enough to make the fuel last. The story of Doolittle's Raiders is one such story.

On April 18, 1942, sixteen B-25 bombers took off from the aircraft carrier, *USS Hornet*, to bomb Tokyo a few months after Pearl Harbor was attacked. Bombers had never been launched from an aircraft carrier before, so these planes had to be modified to in order to make the mission work. All sixteen B-25 bombers, had their heavy guns removed, along with the ammunition and anything else that was deemed unnecessary. They essentially became defenseless, in order to be used as instruments of defense! The lighter weight would allow for a longer distance in flight and the conservation of fuel. They already knew they were not going to return to the carrier, and had to land in China after the raid. They had to give away weight and protection, in order to gain distance and success.

The kingdom of God is like that. We have to choose to give up in order to gain. What God may have to "unload" from our lives, we gain through Jesus over the long haul. Jesus said in Matthew 10:39, "He who has found his life shall lose it, and he who has lost his life for My sake shall find it." To gain we must give away. We must drop and discontinue the way we do life, and ask Jesus to save us and make our lives pleasing to Him. When we accept Christ, we are essentially saying, "Jesus, my life is not mine any longer –– it is now Yours. Do with me as You desire, because I know You know best and You can do better than I can with my life." An old advertising slogan once stated, "Have it your way." That came from Burger King, not the King of Kings! God declared in Isaiah 55:8, "For My thoughts are not your thoughts, nor are your ways My ways." Flynn writes:

> If our main goal in life is to selfishly gain popularity, possessions, and position, we'll miss the higher values of life, and suffer dissatisfaction. But if we set our affection on Christ and things above, we'll discover the abundant life. We lose by finding. We live by dying. (Flynn 1987, 61)

Also, with aspects and possessions of life, are we measuring our worth based upon what we own? I heard a recent radio commercial ask, "Will another pair of shoes make you a better person? Of course not" is the given answer on the commercial. Do we hold onto things assuming they will benefit us, or are we willing to lighten our load to benefit others and ultimately experience success? Had the B-25s not lightened their load, they would have not been able to complete their mission. Do we want to be blessed? Do we want to complete our mission? Then we need to bless others. Jesus said, "If you wish to be complete, go and sell your possessions and give to the poor, and you will have treasure in heaven; and come follow Me" (Matt. 19:21). We will reap what we sow. However, the attitude in this upside-down issue is of critical importance.

The following poem, "The Conquerors" written by Charles Ross Weede, is poignant in this discussion as it contrasts Alexander the Great and Jesus.

THE CONQUERORS

Jesus and Alexander died at thirty-three.
One lived and died for self; one died for you and me;
The Greek died on a throne; the Jew died on a cross;
One's life a triumph seemed; the other but a loss.
One led vast armies forth; the other walked alone.
One shed a whole world's blood; the other gave His own.
One won the world in life and lost it all in death;
The other lost His life to win the whole world's faith.

Jesus and Alexander died at thirty-three.
One died in Babylon, and one on Calvary.
One gained all for himself; and one Himself He gave,
One conquered every throne; the other every grave.
The one made himself God, the God made Himself less,
The one lived but to blast, the other but to bless.
When died the Greek, forever fell his throne of swords;
But Jesus died to live forever Lord of lords.

Jesus and Alexander died at thirty-three.
The Greek made all men slaves; the Jew made all men free.
One built a throne on blood; the other built on love.

The one was born of earth; the other from above.

One won all this earth, to lose all earth and heaven.

The other gave up all, that all to Him be given.

The Greek forever died; the Jew forever lives.

He loses all who gets, and wins all things who gives.

If we are giving to or blessing others just so that we can be blessed, then we are not operating with a kingdom mind-set. We are often *expecting* to get something in return. If true, we are operating ultimately with a "receiving" attitude and an entitlement expectation. When we give, we need to "give it away" or "release it," otherwise it is not giving. We need to understand that if we *expect* something in return, from a person or even from God, we are essentially loaning not giving. While it is true that God blesses when we bless others, what we receive in return is always more than what the world can give.

Essentially, we must die to self in order to truly have life. Jesus said, "For whoever wishes to save his life shall lose it; but whoever loses his life for my sake will find it" (Matt. 16:25). The entitlement, self-centered mindset our culture has been living with today has increasingly resisted the understanding and need for God. As long as we hold onto our lives, as if we know what is best, we will experience death with no life afterward. To live in the Kingdom of God is to lay down our life of selfishness, sin, and rebellion, and be resurrected by the power of Jesus towards true life. True life comes from resurrection. In other words, we must die first before we can truly live.

One can only be resurrected if one is dead. It takes the voice of the Lord Jesus to raise us from the dead. The story of Lazarus, as recorded in John 11:1--46, is an example. After Lazarus died, Jesus came to be with the family, went to the tomb where Lazarus was buried, and cried out, "Lazarus, come forth!" (John 11:43). New life comes through Christ. When we surrender, He will call out to us, "(Your name), come forth!" We have already been given more than we deserve, when we consider salvation through the life, death, and resurrection of Jesus.

Foolishness vs. Wisdom

Understanding the difference between wisdom and foolishness may not be as difficult as other upside-down kingdom concepts. In biblical language, the concept of understanding has much to do with wisdom. Psalm 53:1--2 says,

> The fool has said in his heart, "There is no God," they are corrupt, and have committed abominable injustice; There is no one who does good. God has looked down from heaven upon the sons of men, to see if there is anyone who understands, who seeks after God.

The Hebrew word rendered "understanding" here, means "acts wisely." When understanding is attained, a person makes good choices. The person sees a larger picture and possibly future ramifications. Foolishness is equated to, corruption; decisions based upon emotions such as fear, bitterness, and anger; immaturity or inexperience; being too quick to act or speak; bad choices; and immorality. Wisdom corresponds to seeking after God: "The fear of the Lord is the beginning of wisdom, and the knowledge of the Holy One is understanding" (Prov. 9:10).

On the other hand, many people make decisions through the understanding in their own eyes. Second Timothy 3:1--9 gives a synopsis of many attitudes that contribute to a lack of understanding in our day and in the last days (more on this later). One of the prevailing attitudes is conceit (v. 4). The Greek word here means "wrapped up in smoke." What a great word picture! Arrogance and high-mindedness prevents understanding because they cloud a person's perception and sight because he or she is self-centered. In contrast, the "foolishness" of dependency upon Jesus clears the way for correct perspectives and true understanding.

In Paul's first letter to the Corinthians, he discusses the wisdom of God as it is often in contrast to the wisdom of the world. He states:

> Has God not made foolish the wisdom of the world? For since in the wisdom of God the world through its wisdom did not come to know God, God was well-pleased through the foolishness of the message preached to save those who believe. For indeed Jews ask for signs, and Greeks search for wisdom; but we preach Christ crucified, to Jews a stumbling block, and to Gentiles foolishness, but to those who are the called, both Jews and Greeks, Christ the power of God and the wisdom of God. Because the foolishness of God is wiser than men, and the weakness of God is stronger than men (I Cor. 1:20--25).

Of course there is neither weakness nor foolishness in God, but Paul was simply making a hypothetical contrast. If we are trying to understand God according to the earthly, human wisdom, we will surely miss the mark. It is essential to trust God, even if we do not understand what He may be doing. That is where faith begins.

Church as a Refuge vs. Church as an Army

Jesus declared to His disciples, "Upon this rock I will build my church and the gates of Hell cannot stand against it" (Matt. 16:18). This verse, and others, paints the picture that the church is a moving, growing organism, not just a dormant, static entity. Unfortunately, the Christian church in our society has become one of dormancy, powerlessness, and overly tolerant. The Greek word for church here, "ecclesiasticus," is used mostly to describe a legislative branch who establishes the moral and legal compass for a group or society. "Gates" are where the legislators gather to produce such direction for the people and the world.

The church is like an embassy –– it provides kingdom rule where it exists. For example, an American embassy in another country is considered "American soil." Anyone who visits or occupies the embassy has to live by the laws of that embassy's country even though it is among a foreign land. A citizen can find "sanctuary" in the embassy of their country, even though it rests in another nation. If someone was in trouble in the foreign country, they can go to the embassy of their own country, where the laws of their country prevail, and be safe.

The church is a sanctuary as well, for people willing to find a refuge from the kingdom of darkness. Proverbs 18:10 states, "The Name of the Lord is a strong tower; the righteous runs into it and is safe." In ancient biblical history, cities of refuge had some poignant characteristics. The roads to these cities were always kept open. The avenger could not harm a sinner while in the city of refuge, as long as he stayed in the city. If he left the city, the avenger could have access to him, and even kill him. The sinner had to remain in the city until the high priest died – He was then declared innocent and free to go home! What an amazing picture of the church for all sinners.

The New Testament continues with the description of the church in Hebrews 6:18––20:

... we may have strong encouragement, we who have fled
for refuge in laying hold of the hope set before us. This
hope we have as an anchor of the soul, a hope both sure
and steadfast and one which enters within the veil, where
Jesus has entered as a forerunner for us, having become a
high priest forever . . .

The sinner can "run" from guilt, death, further corruption, and
abuse, and toward safety, healing, help, and restoration. The church
is not an exclusive club –– it is a place of refuge for the hurting and
the sinner.

At the same time, the church's God-given mission is to expand
her influence wherever it is in order to provide a greater place of
grace and sanctification from the sin, death, and destruction of the
kingdom of darkness. The church is a refuge, but it is also on the
move, through its embassies, to influence the rule of hell. The gates
of hell are on the defensive –– the church is on the offensive to bring
God's kingdom rule to the earth –– on earth as it is in heaven.

However, unlike military armies that go on the offensive to win
a battle and the war, the offensive in the kingdom of God is related
to lifestyle. Jesus taught that believers are to be the "salt of the earth"
and "the light of the world" (Matt. 5:13––15). Preaching the gospel to
all nations is a mandate, but our actions and demeanor are supposed
to be consistent with our message. The exposure of abuses in the
church over the last few decades, of sexual abuse, financial abuse, or
pride, have brought ridicule to the church thereby rendering it less
effective and seen with suspicion and indignation. God presence is
a safe place of love, healing, and correction, not harm. Consider the
following:

- Let your light shine before men in such a way that they may see your good works, and glorify your Father who is in heaven. (Matt. 5:16)
- Do all things without grumbling or disputing; that you may prove yourselves to be blameless and innocent, children of God above reproach in the midst of a crooked and perverse generation, among whom you appear as lights in the world. (Phil. 2:14--15)
- Beloved, I urge you as aliens and strangers to abstain from fleshly lusts, which wage war against the soul. Keep your behavior excellent among the Gentiles, so that in the thing in which they slander you as evildoers, they may on account of your good deeds, as they observe them, glorify God in the day of visitation. (1Pet. 2:11--12)

Worldly forces and the forces of Satan resist the church in her endeavor to spread God's ways upon the earth. Throughout history, there were times when men and governments attempted to destroy the church, but God always raised someone up to protect and restore it. For example, the Roman Emperor Domitian (AD 81-96) persecuted Christian believers with the intent of eliminating the church. In AD 303 Emperor Diocletian's first "Edict against the Christians" was published. According to the writings of Eusebius, a Roman Christian historian of that time, the edict ordered the destruction of Christian scriptures, liturgical books, and places of worship across the empire, including any house in which scriptures were found. Eventually, Diocletian also prohibited Christians from assembling for worship.

Christians were also deprived of the right to petition the courts, and could not respond to actions brought against them in court. Christian senators, veterans, and soldiers were deprived of their ranks, and freedmen were once again turned into slaves because of their Christian faith. For the next few years, the church was reeling and almost destroyed. However, in AD 313, the years of Christian persecution came to an end when Emperor Constantine (AD 289-337) issued the Edict of Milan which formally established freedom and acceptance for all religions, including Christianity. As a result, the church was not just restored, but it grew among the nations.

Today, there is an emerging sense of a growing resistance to Christian believers. Faith-based values, especially in the counseling, social work, marketplace, and military environments, are increasingly being eliminated and the related professionals and military chaplains are less able to freely invoke the name of Jesus, the Bible, or Christian values. As a result, we are seeing a crisis in good leadership and moral values. For example, one study has found nearly three-quarters (72 percent) of the public thinks religion is losing influence in America, up from 52 percent who said so in 2002, and most people who say religion's influence is waning see this as a bad thing (Pew Research Center Online, 2014).

For licensed professionals, the threat of losing one's license is now legislated and real, if Christian values are used. Schools have become hostile to any expression of Christian values, yet other values like Muslim and pagan views are conveyed. We are indeed in a spiritual battle. However, unless Jesus returns soon, the ultimate victory will be what the true church has to offer. For as in other times in history, man's and Satan's attempt to eradicate the Christian church will fail, and the church will once again be sought out for help. In the days that lie ahead, the power of the Holy Spirit will be what draws many to the truth, since He will contrast the powers of the world. When all else fails, God's truth will prevail.

In contemporary Christendom, a dichotomy often occurs. Some

Christian churches and denominations emphasize a "social gospel," where the helping of the disenfranchised is the main mission. Mercy and grace are expressed through community building, peacemaking, and generosity. As such, the church stands out as a resource for justice and mercy. Many such churches are criticized for their approach, because they are seen to be too passive and as tolerating sin and unrighteousness.

Other churches and denominations choose to emphasize the righteousness of God and the complete conversion of a person's soul as a means to obtain the assistance that is needed. True conversion is seen as a means to righteous living and better decision making, thereby positively affecting communities in a more sustainable way over time. The transformation that takes place in individuals causes them to become more like Christ and therefore empowers them to live a life of righteousness and better decision-making. This positively impacts not just the individual's life, but the community as well. However, such churches are often viewed as unapproachable and uncaring of the needs of their community.

Both sides of this Christian expression have their merits and truths, and together, they need to convey the complete heart of God. I believe that in the days that lie ahead, this dichotomy will diminish as the church experiences growing persecution. Then we will all be compelled to show forth the united aspects of God in order to survive and make a powerful difference in the increasingly evil world. Persecution will never destroy the church, for the gates of hell shall never overpower the church (Matt. 16:18). Persecution will always make the church unified and stronger. The power of God is shown in love and mercy as well as righteousness and truth.

Understanding God through Encounters

In many of the old cartoons and the newspaper comic strips, we may remember times when characters had a moment of enlightenment -- a moment when they had an idea or came to a great understanding. When that occurred, we would see a light bulb flick on over their head at that moment as a sign of clarity. We may use that colloquialism today when discussing a moment of understanding in another individual or ourselves. We often say, "The light bulb just went on." Another way of describing a moment of understanding is declaring, "I just had an 'ah-ha' moment." There are many times we have experienced such moments, and when we do, we have gained either a small or a great understanding of a person or a situation. Ah-ha moments bring understandings that have a tendency to stick with us because of the impact and emotions that maybe attached to them.

The Bible presents many such moments in the lives of the people of the Old or New Testaments. I would like to briefly discuss three stories that reveal times where a person dramatically understands a life-changing aspect. Sometimes understanding may not be achieved until a life-changing occurrence take place. However, arriving at an understanding does not have to take place through dramatic experiences. If we are teachable and humble, we can possess understanding more readily.

One of my favorite Bible accounts is that of the man born blind as recorded in John 9. The story is rich with insights. This man was healed by Jesus and had gained his sight. The people who knew this blind man were amazed at his healing. The story indicates that the community knew the blind man and his parents for a long time. Once he was healed and gained his sight, the man's neighbors began to ask him many questions. The man simply described the scene in which Jesus healed him and how it was done.

The neighbors then brought the man to the Pharisees, attempting to obtain an explanation as to how his healing could be possible. The religious leaders also had difficulty explaining the man's healing, and continued asking many questions, including what he knew about Jesus. Not satisfied with his answers and doubting his story, John 9:18 reads, "The Jews therefore did not believe it of him, that he had been blind, and had received sight, until they called the parents of the very one who had received his sight." So the parents became part of the inquisition, and they confirmed that the man was their son, that he was born blind, and that they did not know how it could be that he gained his sight.

As we read the entire story in chapter 9 of John, several things emerge. Many people, including the religious leaders, could not believe that this man was healed of his blindness. The people and the leaders also tried to discredit the man and his story. The people and the leaders tried to discredit Jesus as well, suggesting that only Moses was credible to them, and Jesus was a fraud. The spirit of this story is that agendas and assumptions were being challenged, and the healing of the man born blind was undermining the set assumptions of the day. The man became exasperated by the insistent inquisition and attitudes of the religious leaders, and his inability to answer all their petty questions. The man finally declared with authority and conviction: "One thing I do know. I was blind but now I see!"(John 9:25, NIV).

Understanding is often much more simple than we make it out to be. We may have an obvious situation, yet our prejudices and assumptions cloud the simplicity of the truth (more on this in a later chapter). Sometimes we may even refuse the truth (like the Pharisees did and many "religious" people do today), which hinders the understanding altogether. This story of the healed blind man illustrates the simplicity of a dramatic experience that led to a basic declaration, "I may not be able to answer all your intricate questions but, I was blind and now I see! That is all I know! And Jesus was the one who did it!" The healed blind man didn't care what else he needed to explain about the situation, the technique Jesus used, or about Jesus Himself. His "ah-ha" moment was the ability to declare the simple truth that he now could see. That is all he needed to understand.

Today we have disputes over whether God can still do miracles, signs, and wonders. Some religious people are often so resistant to the supernatural, that they may miss what God has for them. God is not natural. He is by nature supernatural (although to Him, He is naturally God), especially compared to the created world. The religious leaders of the Bible story were so caught up in interrogating the healed blind man, that they missed the fact that he was a healed blind man! "But avoid foolish controversies and genealogies and strife and disputes about the Law, for they are unprofitable and worthless" (Titus 3:9).

Also, Colossians 2:8 states, "See to it that no one takes you captive through philosophy and empty deception, according to the tradition of men, according to the elementary principles of the world, rather than according to Christ." The love, power, and presence of God are aspects that cannot be encapsulated or explained away. To do so places us in a position of greater ability than God. We understand God because of His presence and His interventions in the lives of human beings, not only through His Word.

The story of the woman at the well, as recorded in John 4, is another example of an episodic moment of understanding. The story is about a Samaritan woman who encounters Jesus at a well on His way to Galilee. At first the conversation is taking place on two different planes, if you will. She is speaking with an understanding of the practical, and Jesus is speaking with a spiritual understanding. Something that all of us can relate to, I'm sure. He asks her for a drink, and she wonders why He is even having a conversation with a Samaritan since the Jews would not interface with them. He describes a well that can give "living water" (v. 10). She keeps the dialog in a practical sense, observing that Jesus has no bucket or anyway to draw from a well of any kind. Jesus continues with the reference to Himself as "the well" that gives out living water that never runs dry and brings eternal life (v. 14). She then asks, "Sir give me this water, so I will not be thirsty, nor come all the way here to draw" (v. 15).

Jesus asks her to get her husband and come back. The woman says she had no husband. Jesus responds, "You have well said, 'I have no husband', for you have had five husbands, and the one whom you now have is not your husband; this you have said truly" (v. 17–-18). At this point, the woman has an "ah-ha" moment and understands something about the man she is speaking to. "Sir, I perceive that you are prophet" (v. 19). She understood that there was something different about Jesus. He was more than just a man sitting near a well. He called her out, but she didn't feel judged. Interestingly, the conversation continued regarding the proper way to worship. Jesus states, "You worship that which you do not know; we worship that which we know" (v. 22). He then declares to her that He is the long-awaited Messiah (vs. 25-26).

Why is this important? The woman discovered a God who knew about her -- including her sin -- and yet did not feel put off. Jesus was attempting to introduce her to a God she could know, who knew all about her, and yet she could worship "in spirit and in truth" (v. 24). Worshiping the Lord is not just about style, tradition, type of music, ritual, or in a certain type of building. Jesus stated that we need to worship that which we know -- a God who is intimate with us knowing our weaknesses and sins, and who desires us to be intimate with Him –– not something or someone we don't know. Most people fall under the latter category. Despite the woman's confession of Jesus being a prophet, He declared He was much more than that, which transitioned into the discussion of the focus of worship.

Similarly, Paul had an opportunity to speak to religious leaders in Athens, who worshiped many idols. Acts 17:16––34 records this encounter. The men ask Paul to tell them about Jesus and the resurrection. He observed that they were "very religious in all respects" (Acts 17:22). He then acknowledged, "I also found an altar with this inscription, 'TO AN UNKNOWN GOD.' What therefore you worship in ignorance, this I proclaim to you" (Acts 17:23). The rest of chapter 17 in Acts records Paul describing Jesus as the "unknown God." As I discussed in the first chapter of this book, Jesus helps us understand God, because of His appearing in the flesh and having dwelt among us. We can know God through Jesus.

We no longer have to worship a God we do not know. God is not so distant and hidden as we tend to make Him. He knows us intimately, yet desires relationship with us. Can we worship a God who knows us, calls us out regarding sin, and does so because He loves us enough to see us in a better light than we see ourselves? Or would we feel judged and question whether He loved us? It is critical to understand that God does not condemn those who belong to Him, and He will seek to correct and guide from a standpoint of love. Such correction comes from the great loving parent, who has our best in mind.

Finally, we will consider the story of the prodigal son, as recorded in Luke 15. A man had two sons. The younger son asked his father for his share of the estate right away, while his father was still living. In the ancient cultures, such a thing would be like wishing one's father was dead –– it was more than just asking for his share of the inheritance. The son was expressing rejection of the father and yet wanted his money.

The parable continues with how the son "squandered his estate with loose living" (v. 13) to the point that he had nothing. In his broken state, the son asked for a job to feed swine (to the Jewish mind, a desperate and despicable option indeed). As the son was feeding the swine, he resorted to eating the swine food as well. Then it hit him. His "ah-ha" moment occurred.

The son realized, despite how he felt about his father, he never had it so good. He realized that his life on the plantation was not so bad after all, since even his father's servants lived a better life than he was living at his current place and time (v.17). He decided to humble himself and go home, to repent, face his father, and hope for the best (vs. 18-19). As he traveled home, the son most likely reflected on the many things he took for granted and how he squandered what his father gave him. He surely did not expect what would happen as he came closer to home.

Verse 20 says, "But while he was still *a long way off*, his father saw him, and felt compassion for him, *and ran* and embraced him, and kissed him" (italics mine). We are all a "long way off" from relationship with God the Father because of sin, rebellion, and separation. Yet God the Father sees us and pursues us! He understands our state, and wants to take the initiative to do something about it. The prodigal son's father ran to him to welcome him home. But, the son had to decide to turn himself back home. The son's new understanding of what his father and his home meant to him caused a reconciliation and celebration. Episodic understandings are life changing and once an "ah-ha" moment takes place, we not only gain understanding, but we change the way we make decisions and as well as our perspectives.

These are just a few Bible stories that exemplify changed lives due to new understanding of God. However, there are many examples of Bible stories and life occurrences that make it difficult to understand God. The next chapter will briefly address some areas in which God seems so distant and hard to understand.

CHAPTER 3
Understanding Difficult Biblical Teachings

The fear of the Lord is the beginning of wisdom, and
the knowledge of the Holy One is understanding.

-- Proverbs 9:10

Jesus said to them, 'If God were your father, you
would love Me, for I proceed forth and have come from
God . . . why do you not understand what I am saying?
It is because you cannot hear My word . . . But because I
speak the truth, you do not believe Me.

-- John 8:42--45

I have heard it said that the English language is a difficult language
to learn, because of things like synonyms, figures of speech,
and the many similar sounding words that have different meanings.
Words like *house* and *home* are used interchangeably, but can also be
seen as having slightly different meanings. Figures of speech can
be especially difficult to someone who is learning our language. For
example, "racking our brains" is a figure of speech, that does not

have a direct translation from another language, causing a potential misunderstanding of the phrase. Finally, similar sounding words like *their* and *there*, and *to* and *too*, can be misused, and are often misspelled in writing, causing additional confusion in communication.

I am sure we all have often heard that God's Word can be hard to understand, or that there are contradictions to it. We may have wondered about a lot of biblical stories and concepts as well. The truth is, it may not occur that our limited finite minds will *completely* grasp all that God is saying and doing, short of divine revelation, while we are living on earth. However, the Word reveals more than enough for us to understand a holy God, a loving God, a righteous God, a redeeming God, and an active, intimate God. Faith is then required in order for us to trust God for the rest of what we do not understand about Him and His ways. In addition, like with any other relationship, the more we spend time with God and His Word, the more we understand Him. Hebrews 11:1 says, "Now faith is the assurance of things hoped for, the conviction of things not seen." We will discuss the aspect of conviction as it relates to understanding in a later chapter.

Many times, loss, suffering, trials, abuse, and consequences of our decisions can place doubt and even rejection in our minds about God and His goodness. Military men and women who return from combat experience will sometimes question God and the meaning of life. The moral guilt and combat trauma that they experienced can be overwhelming. Spouses and children, who go through a divorce or the death of their husband/wife or parent, often feel abandoned, wondering if anyone understands them. Victims of abuse are left feeling like they are "throw-aways" and no one knows their plight.

We often feel God is too silent in areas where we believe His attention is needed. Frankly, it is indeed difficult to sometimes reconcile what we are experiencing with the stated truths of God found in the Bible. One only has to read many of the Psalms, the books of Lamentations, the book of Job, and Ecclesiastes to see that human kind throughout history has had similar questions about life and God, which were often not answered, at least in the way and time people needed them.

I recently read a story that provides a testimony to this discussion. In a *Voice of the Martyrs* (VOM) newsletter, a story of a family in the country of Colombia was presented, where a decade-long civil war left many victims. Rebel groups singled out and murdered Christians, leaving many grieving widows and children behind.

> Luz, who was eight months pregnant with twins, had just moved to a small FARC (Revolutionary Armed Forces of Columbia)-controlled village with her husband, Diego, and their young daughter so Diego could pastor a dying church there. One night, Diego and others traveled to the nearby town of El Dovio to buy a microphone for an upcoming youth prayer meeting. After arriving in the town, they were stopped by four FARC guerillas who asked to see their IDs. Diego didn't have his with him, but he hoped they would be appeased by learning he was a pastor. They weren't. Instead, they abducted him. Two days later, Diego's dismembered body was found in a trash bag. "A lot of times I've asked, 'Why?' she told a VOM worker tearfully. "I ask, 'If we were faithful, why did You allow this to happen to me?'" By God's grace and with VOM's support, Luz has grown through her grief, experienced healing and continued on with her life. Luz and her children, now 9 and 7 (twins), (live in) a safe house in another part of Columbia. However, the children do miss not knowing their dad. "It's been really hard," Luz

said. "Even our little girl . . . keeps asking about her daddy. She says that she wants to see him one day. There's a lot of things here that we don't understand as humans, but one day we'll understand them when we're before our Lord." (VOM, 2016, pages 4–5).

I acknowledge that it is difficult to go into theological and doctrinal depths to help explain things like suffering, evil in the world, God's silence, and so forth. There are many other resources that provide a deeper discussion than I am prepared to do here (see appendix). But I also know this: even when resources address such deep and difficult aspects of our faith, they are still often found to be lacking. We want answers when we have none. We want solutions when we experience difficult times. We simply want someone, anyone, to understand how we feel and come along side us. Our cry may simply be, "Can someone just understand how I feel right now?"

Human nature also wants to be "in the know." What we don't know, we tend to reject. What we don't fully understand, we tend to question. Questions and exploration are legitimate pursuits –– since that is how we often find answers and gain understanding. But if we question with the attitude of cynicism and with the intent of discarding, we will not come to the truth. If we ever claimed we know as much as God knew, He would cease to be God. That may be a difficult admission, but it is a necessary understanding.

One of the attractive lies to Adam and Eve in the garden of Eden was the claim from the serpent that if they simply took from the forbidden tree, the tree of the *Knowledge* of Good and Evil, their "eyes will be opened, and you will be like God, knowing good and evil" (Gen. 3:5). That is still a temptation for all of us today –– to take for ourselves what appears to be the ways to obtain wisdom and understanding –- instead of depending on God to reveal to us what we need to know when we need to know it. Can we leave with God His prerogative to give and provide understanding in His time for our benefit?

Eve even admitted that the "tree was desirable to make one wise" and took from it (Gen. 3:6). Did it make them any wiser? Apparently not. In fact, Adam blamed Eve and God, and Eve blamed the serpent, (Gen. 3:12–-13) as if they had no choice. Sure, it is desirable, and even selfishly satisfying to obtain "ill-gotten gain" of any kind –- material things as well as information. Can we be content in waiting?

Consider how often each news media station will clamor to be the first to "break the news" about anything, and may even speculate at times, just to make it seem as if they know something more than another reporter or station. And we drink it up, just to be in the know. Can we be content with what we presently know, work within it and be faithful? Heaven forbid that we have to admit at times, "I don't know." Having knowledge does not always translate into understanding and wisdom. The alternative posture of waiting and being faithful with what we do have is a humbling one to take indeed. Where God gives grace to be humble, He will also give wisdom, faith, and holiness.

The Bible says that Adam's and Eve's eyes were opened indeed (Gen. 3:7) but what they saw led to shame, guilt, blaming others, rebellion, a distrust of each other and of God, contentiousness, and envy that eventually resulted in the first murder –- Cain killing his brother Abel (Gen. 4:1–-10). Not the most desirable outcomes of always seeking to be in the know, if you ask me. Selfishly obtaining understanding is bad enough, but it is the striving and contentious energies that says, "I gotta know more than you and before you do" or "I gotta have what you have or get it before you get it" that really gets us in trouble. The remedy is to cast our care upon God, and leave every event to His wise and gracious disposal. Proverbs 9:10 says, "The fear (honor; respect; reverence) of the Lord is the beginning of wisdom, and the knowledge of the Holy One is understanding." We are called to start with a relationship with God, and He will reveal to us more than we can ever gain for ourselves –- in due time (1Pet. 5:6). For our eyes to be opened, we simply need to ask:

> But if any of you lacks wisdom, let him ask of God, who gives to all men generously and without reproach, and it will be given to him. But let him ask in faith without any doubting, for the one who doubts is like the surf of the sea driven and tossed by the wind. For let not that man expect that he will receive anything from the Lord, being a double-minded man, unstable in all his ways. . . Do not be deceived, my beloved brethren. Every good thing bestowed and every perfect gift is from above, coming down from the father of lights, with whom there is no variation, or shifting shadow (James 1:5–-8, 16–-17).

When we encounter trials, disappointments, and tragedy, we commonly ask, "Why?" We all want to know, "Why me?" or "What did I do to deserve this?" These are difficult questions to answer, and we often do not receive the answers we seek. We simply just want to understand. It is natural to ask these questions, but can we remain tenacious and steadfast in the midst of silence? It is in moments like these that we walk away from God, break relationships, and act out in anger. Not knowing, when we feel we need to know, is difficult for most people.

Since evil and suffering in our world are a result of either the choices that men and women make, or the fact that we are in a fallen, broken world (which incidentally, came to be because of a man's and a woman's choice to turn away from God in the first place), we must keep in mind that if we want God to remove despair from the world, then He would also have to remove our free will. God gave us the ability to choose, and when we do not follow His ways, pain, disappointment, tragedy, and offenses take place. We can choose to do harm or we can choose to be a blessing.

Jesus lamented over His people when He observed their sin and rejection of God: "O Jerusalem, Jerusalem who kills the prophets and stones those who are sent to her! How often I wanted to gather your children together, the way a hen gathers her chicks under her wings, and you were unwilling" (Matt. 23:37). God does not violate our will to choose, but He can transform a person's "data base" from where an individual makes choices, if we invite Him to do so. Even in that case, we have to choose to accept Jesus and allow the Holy Spirit to influence our lives.

If you are a parent, think of how often you had a similar lament as Jesus. I can remember saying to myself, and at times to my children, "If only you had listened to us." "If only you made your decision based upon what you knew to be true." "If only you allowed me to help you." The inference is that the source of wisdom and understanding (God, parents, the Bible, caring mature people, etc.) are not being heard enough. The resulting choices turn into undesired outcomes that cause hurt, rejection, disappointments, and destruction. We often have no one else to blame but ourselves, yet we blame God and others.

But there is good news! Despite the tendency to hear nothing but bad news on the media outlets, there is much more going on than we understand. Even in the midst of dysfunction, there is hope. Even when there is brokenness there can be restoration. That is where the redemption power of Jesus can take over. Often, He is working His good and restorative power behind the scenes. "Look among the nations! Observe! Be astonished! Wonder! Because I am doing something in your days – you would not believe it if you were told" (Hab. 1:5).

He is also working according to His time. "For the vision is yet for the appointed time; it hastens toward the goal, and it will not fail. Though it tarries, wait for it; for it will certainly come, it will not delay" (Hab. 2:3). God often works "suddenly," and we may feel things take so long. Will we even recognize when God "suddenly" shows up or works something out? When God's redemption and restoration occur, the groundswell is usually more than enough to overcome the pain of the past. The hope in Jesus is for the taking, even when we do not understand the situation. Often, hope is all we have to hold onto.

We also underestimate the spiritual warfare that takes place against us. If we desire to follow God and His calling in our lives, we can especially expect the devil to resist, thwart, and hurt us in our endeavors. The ways that Satan may choose to come against us may not always appear to make sense. We may not "connect the dots" during a disappointing or even destructive experience, to see that the devil was behind the situation. We may blame God for our experiences, when it may in fact be our adversary. The devil hates God, and therefore, he hates the people of God. In times like this, it is difficult to understand what is happening behind the scenes.

Job was a man who was traumatized and suffered greatly. He lost his seven sons and three daughters, his cattle, his servants, his wealth, and his health -- all within a day's time. His wife cried out to Job that he should, "curse God and die" (Job 2:9). He had no idea that spiritual warfare was taking place. For some reason, God chose to not reveal that to Job. Did he have complete understanding of what was occurring? No, Job had no idea what was going on behind the scenes. Not an easy place to be.

Many of us, and many people to whom we minister, have similar life situations with no explanation. Yet, despite Job's pain, discouragement, and bad advice from his friends, he held onto what he knew *about* God, as rickety as that may have been -- "Through all this Job did not sin nor did he blame God" (Job 1:22). He did eventually question God, as most of us would in circumstances much less than what he experienced. At the end of the story, and *through his pain*, God speaks to him to correct and encourage him. It is important to note that correction can also be encouragement -- something I believe we overlook today (more on that in a later chapter). It is at that point that Job makes a powerful confession of repentance. Job 42:2--5 records his response to God:

> I know that You can do all things; no plan of Yours can be thwarted. You asked, "Who is this that obscures my counsel without knowledge?" Surely I spoke of things I did not understand, things too wonderful for me to know. You said, "Listen now, and I will speak; I will question you, and you shall answer Me." My ears had *heard* of You but now my eyes have *seen* You. (NIV, *italics* mine)

Understanding God and His ways comes through reading His Word, revelation, experience, and time with Him. Understanding God often increases through times of trials, disappointments, and pain -- sometimes with more impact than through miracles, signs, and wonders. Essentially, it is not enough to just know about God -- we need to encounter Him!

Jesus can relate as well. While He was praying just before He was arrested and put on trial, He declared, "My soul is overwhelmed with sorrow to the point of death" (Matt. 26:38, NIV). Someone who may be so depressed can have thoughts like this. When Jesus was on the cross, close to death, He cried out, "My God, My God, why hast though forsaken me?" (Matt. 27:46). Jesus experienced such inner turmoil that He too wondered where God was. Notice, He did not say "Father, Father. . ." Relationship with His Father seemed broken and so distant at this point. He cried as most of us would, "My God, why. . .?" (And we can fill in the blank with any of our life hurts.)

The death of a loved one, divorce, unemployment, betrayal, illness and weakness, financial difficulties, childhood abuse, sexual assault, broken relationships, depression, or destruction of property are just a few of many life experiences that can devastate us in this life. We often wonder "Where is God?" in times like these. We do not understand why God would allow these things to happen in our lives. When we don't understand something or someone, our tendency is to reject, become anxious or angry, blame others, shun others, and isolate ourselves. We often blame God and isolate ourselves from Him. There comes a point where we are either becoming "bitter or better." Bitterness blinds us. "Betterness" grows us.

Just before He died, Jesus said, "It is finished" (John 19:30). Through the process of grief and struggles, we need to arrive at a point where we cease our striving for answers. Even if we were to receive answers, it may not always be what actually settles us anyway. We arrive at a place of surrender, to be finished with the despair of not understanding, leading to peace, even if we do not have a complete understanding. This is an important and essential place at which to arrive.

After the "Why?" question, are we able to cease our mental and emotional struggle for answers, and say, "It is finished"? We need to finish our striving. Can we stop trying so hard to find answers, and simply settle into the hands of God? That is what Jesus did, when His last words were, "Father, into Thy hands I commit My spirit" (Luke 23:46). The best place to be is in the restful hands of God, especially if we do not understand what is going on. Psalm 46:10 (KJV) declares, "Be still and know that I am God." Run to Him, and you will find rest for your soul.

Until Jesus returns, we will continue to be exposed to the brokenness of this sinful world and its effects. Jesus has promised that when He returns, He will set things straight and back to what existed before sin and rebellion occurred. Even now, the *entire* creation "groans" while we wait for the restoration of all things (Rom. 8:18–-25).

When we are no longer able to do what needs to be done by our own assessment, our dependency upon God tends to grow. Social analysts point out that people turn to religion in times of crisis and instability. The terrorist attacks on September 11, 2001, certainly shattered the stability and comfort of Americans' lives, leading to a surge in church attendance and Bible sales immediately after the attacks. Interesting how that works. We all have an innate sense when difficult and devastating times occur that we need to seek something or someone beyond ourselves for comfort and hope. It is a shame that we seek God only when we need Him. The Lord desires relationship with us so we can experience His presence and love simply because we walk with Him daily.

The more we depend upon God, the greater comfort we can experience and the more we understand His love and guidance in our lives. We may still not understand the circumstances, but we can sense His comfort and presence, even where there is no explanation. The more we understand God, the more we are willing to depend upon Him. However, this is a life long journey, and many people do not remain with God for the long haul. We are too quick to bail out when understanding does not occur instantaneously.

We tend to want answers now –– to be in the know –– in our time. We often become discouraged easily when we feel too much time has passed. It is often a growth cycle that the Lord deems necessary for our good. Jeremiah 29:13 says, "And you will seek Me and find Me, when you search for Me with all your heart." He already understands us and He wants us to understand Him –– at least enough to trust Him with our lives.

Daniel was a Jewish youth who remained devoted to God, even in a nation where a decree was created that only the king and his idol image was to be worshiped. It was said of Daniel, as well as Shadrach, Meshach, and Abed-nego that, "God gave them knowledge and intelligence in every branch of literature and wisdom; Daniel even understood all kinds of visions and dreams" (Dan. 1:17). King Nebuchadnezzar had dreams that disturbed him greatly, and no one among his magicians or sorcerers was able to interpret his dreams.

Eventually, Daniel was recognized and called to interpret the dreams (Dan. 2). Not only did he interpret the dream, but he first described the dream to Nebuchadnezzar, without knowing it ahead of time. Upon Daniel's accurate description and interpretation, the king made this statement: "Surely your God is a God of gods and a Lord of kings and a revealer of mysteries" (Dan. 2:47). In order to know what God knows, when He chooses to reveal them in any area of life, a person must be in relationship with Him. What may be mysteries to us at one time may not remain mysteries forever. Understanding is possible.

Spiritual Understandings

The gospels record how often Jesus spoke in such a way that confounded His hearers. He often had to teach them in parables because their spiritual understanding was lacking. Jesus explained, "Therefore I speak to them in parables; because while seeing they do not see, and while hearing they do not hear, nor do they understand" (Matt. 13:13). Jesus would also speak in ways that seemed a bit disturbing, but again He was using spiritual terms.

In John 4, the disciples came back from obtaining some food and asked Jesus to eat. "But he said to them, 'I have food to eat that you do not know about'" (v. 32). The disciples thought Jesus had stashed some food away, or that someone else brought Him something to eat (v. 33). They may have thought Jesus was squirreling food away for Himself and withholding from them. However, Jesus was referring to a different understanding, "Jesus said to them, 'My food is to do the will of Him who sent Me, and to accomplish His work'" (v. 34).

Another time Jesus declared, "He who eats my flesh and drinks my blood has eternal life, and I will raise him up on the last day. For My flesh is true food, and My blood is true drink" (John 6:54–55). Many of His disciples thought Jesus was being literal (v. 60), and as a result, many peeled away and no longer followed Him (v. 66). Difficult statements and difficult times will have the same effect among people who understand only natural and temporal things. It often takes a spiritual mindset to truly understand our life and times.

Finally, during one of Jesus's many encounters with the scribes and Pharisees, He began speaking about death. Jesus stated, "If anyone keeps My word, they will never see death" (John 8:51). The religious leaders argued that Jesus had a demon (v. 52) and that Abraham and the prophets died (v. 54). Jesus was referring to eternal, spiritual death, but the religious leaders understood Him to mean physical death. Once again, a natural mind will often miss the understanding of the things related to spiritual truth.

To truly understand Jesus, we need to have the Holy Spirit, who reveals Christ and spiritual truth. To truly understand the Word of God, it takes the author, the Holy Spirit of God, to reveal to us His meaning while we read it. We often get bogged down in what appears to be meanings based on the vernacular speech at the time, through our current events, or through our language nuances of the time, instead of the unchanging meanings of God.

Allow me to discuss one of the most misunderstood, and anxiety-driven teachings of Jesus. I have spent time in ministry and counseling with many Christians who hold to a fear-based belief regarding the following concept.

The Unforgivable Sin

One of the most common misunderstandings in scripture is related to what Jesus classified as the unforgiveable sin. Christians and non-Christians alike seem to be on edge as to whether they have committed the unforgivable sin in their daily lives. I have counseled many regarding their fear of this sin. Many have speculated as to the true meaning of the unforgiveable sin. Based upon much misunderstanding, many have been kept in bondage and fear.

This sin, the blaspheming of the Holy Spirit, as Jesus spoke of it, is found in Luke 12:10 and as quoted below, in Matthew 12:30–32:

> He who is not with Me is against Me; and he who does not gather with me scatters. Therefore I say to you, and sin and blasphemy shall be forgiven men, but blasphemy against the Spirit shall not be forgiven. And whoever shall speak a word against the Son of man, it shall be forgiven him,

but whoever shall speak against the Holy Spirit, it shall
not be forgiven him, either in this age, or the age to come.

The one Greek word used in the New Testament to describe
blasphemy is *blasphemeo* which means, "to speak with contempt,"
"to defame," and to "speak against God." To speak with contempt
and defamation is to outright reject with hatred. This is a heart
issue. Sometimes we feel God is not with us in times of loss and
pain because of the emotions at the moment. That is not necessarily
the same connotation as the Greek meaning here. The true spirit of
the Greek word is total, decisive rejection of what the Holy Spirit is
trying to reveal to a person. Upon that rejection, we are left in our
sin and unforgiven.

Jesus first makes a distinction between His ministry and the
ministry of the Holy Spirit. God is united in a Trinity and expressed
in three manifestations –– the Father, the Son, and the Holy Spirit.
All show forth aspects of the one God. Those who speak against
the Son would be forgiven –– provided we not reject the Holy Spirit
who reveals Jesus to humankind. We can claim that Jesus was a good
teacher. We can argue that His miracles can be rationally explained
away, and that He was a religious leader. However, once we know
the truth that Jesus is the Messiah and Savior, that He is God and
the only way to heaven, we can be forgiven of our past based upon
our new understanding and confession.

A person only needs to remember Peter. First, he made a powerful
confession about who Jesus was in John 6:69, "And we have believed
and come to know that You are the Holy One of God." Contrary
to popular opinion at the time, Peter also declared in this verse,
"Thou art the Christ, the Son of the living God." Jesus affirmed and
blessed Peter for the revelation of truth. Peter's confession and belief

were sincere, although still being formed. However, he denied Jesus three times, yet he was forgiven and restored. Peter wept bitterly (Matt. 26:75) when he realized what he had done, and Jesus forgave him and chose him to later be a powerful cornerstone of the young Christian church. The point here is that Peter did not turn away the Holy Spirit's revelation of who Jesus was, even though his faith was weak in some areas.

The ministry of the Holy Spirit is different. His primary ministry, among many others, is to reveal the truth, and the reality of God in the person and power of Jesus Christ. In Matthew 16, Jesus was encouraging His disciples about His crucifixion, death and resurrection, and He explained to them the benefits of Him "going away." To return to the Father was more beneficial than remaining on earth:

> But I tell you the truth, it is to your advantage that I go away; for if I do not go away, the Helper (*Holy Spirit*) shall not come to you; but if I go, I will send Him to you. And He, when He comes, will convict the world concerning sin, and righteousness and judgment; concerning sin, because they do not believe Me; and concerning judgment, because the ruler of this world has been judged . . . But when the Spirit of truth comes, He will guide you *into all the truth*; for He will not speak on His own initiative, but whatever He hears he will speak; and He will disclose to you what is to come. He shall glorify Me; for He shall take of Mine and disclose it to you. All things that the Father has are Mine; therefore I said, that He takes of Mine, and will disclose it to you. (Matt. 16:7--11, 13--15)(*italics* mine)

If we decline and deny what the Spirit is revealing to us, we remain unbelievers and mired in our sin, therefore unforgiven before God. The blaspheming of the Holy Spirit is simply when a person denies and rejects the reality of God, as revealed in Jesus Christ, with contempt, hatred, rebellion, defaming, and defiling. Jesus makes it clear in Matthew 15:16–-20:

> Jesus said, "Are you still lacking in understanding also? Do you not understand that everything that goes into the mouth passes into the stomach, and is eliminated? But the things that proceed out of the mouth *come from the heart*, and those defile the man. For out of the heart come evil thoughts, murders, adulteries, fornications, thefts, false witness, slanders (*blasphemeo*). These are the things which defile the man; but to eat with unwashed hands does not defile the man. (*italics* mine)

Essentially, blaspheming is a heart issue that completely rejects Christ. As a result, a person would remain in his or her sin and unforgiven. A born-again, transformed Christian, who also accepts the present ministry of the Holy Spirit, is not in danger of ever committing this unforgiveable sin. It is not the same as questioning God when we are hurting or when we do not understand a difficult or disappointing situation. It is possible to question God, and not reject Him. We can even cry out to God while distraught and not outright reject Him. Those instances are not blaspheming the Holy Spirit. Those who have been made right with God by faith in Christ are not condemned (John 5:24; Rom 8:1–-4; Col 2:14), but those who refuse to believe in Jesus are condemned already (John 3:16–-18; Rom 1:18–-32; Gal 1:8–-9).

We are sanctified and forgiven and established in relationship with God through Jesus. The relationship with Jesus is the crux of the issue. Do not let the devil, or anyone else, try to heap condemnation upon you if you are a Christian because a true Jesus follower cannot be guilty of the unforgivable sin.

The next chapter will discuss an issue that is essential in our understanding of God, ourselves, and the world around us. Perhaps, our ability to develop relationships, make decisions, and rule our lives, our homes, our churches, our communities, and our nations hinges upon our understanding of what will be discussed next.

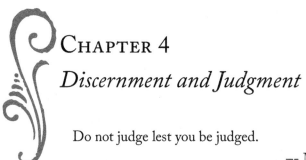

CHAPTER 4

Discernment and Judgment

Do not judge lest you be judged.

-- Matthew 7:1

Or do you not know that the saints will judge the world? And if the world is judged by you, are you not competent to constitute the smallest law courts? Do you not know that we shall judge angels? How much more, matters in this life?

-- 1 Corinthians 6:2-3

He has told you, O man, what is good; and what does the Lord require of you but to do justice, to love kindness, and to walk humbly with your God?

-- Micah 6:8

Brian and Amy came to my office and began to discuss their marriage of two years. "My wife is on my case all the time. I work hard, I am in graduate school, I try to spend time together, but it's never enough for her."

I asked, "What do you understand her beef to be with you?"

"Well, she claims I drink too much." He continued, "I have to have something to kind of take the edge off after a tough day."

"How much alcohol are we talking about," I asked.

"Oh, maybe five to six beers a night, and perhaps more on the weekends, especially when I am over my best friend's house. Really, *not that much.*"

As we continued in our sessions, Brian admitted that his drinking removed himself from time with his wife, as he would pass out after drinking "a few" beers. In addition, his wife looked forward to the weekends together, but he spent time with his buddies instead. Amy, while she needed to address her concern a different way with a different tone, was not judging Brian, as a spouse has the right to express concern over destructive behaviors of their husband or wife. As Brian became aware that his wife was not judging him but rather crying out from a standpoint of love and concern over his increasing drinking, he began to see that he needed some help. He sometimes was aware of how he "dropped the ball" as it related to his relationship with his wife, but because he claimed he was being judged, he continued to resist the need for change in himself.

The previous chapters briefly addressed some difficult issues that sometimes affect our ability to understand, especially as it relates to God. Perhaps one of the most confusing aspects is the distinction between discernment and judgment -- if there is one. I believe that how we feel about this concept will determine our ability to understand and walk in wisdom and conviction.

Dr. James Marcia suggests four statuses of identity, as I mentioned in my book, *Created for Significance* -- Identity Diffusion; Identity Foreclosure; Identity Moratorium; and Identity Achievement (Craig, 1996). Identity diffusion describes a person with no challenges and no convictions, leading to an "anything goes" mindset and no real awareness of identity. Identity foreclosure describes a person with no exploration, but rather having developed an identity dictated to him or her from what others have said, without question. Identity moratorium describes a person in a crisis of life and belief due to many factors, but with no convictions, struggling with no direction as if his or her life is on hold. Lastly, Identity achievement describes someone who has explored, discovered, even through difficult times, and arrived at convictions resulting in an awareness of who he or she is and a committed direction in life. Even though these statuses related mostly to a person's identity and purpose, I believe they can relate to a general and specific spiritual understanding as well.

I believe that diffusion and foreclosure, as it relates to premature identity formation, can also be applied to the spiritual lapse in understanding and how to relate to God, the Bible, and the twenty-first century. The diffusion concept leads to refrain from pursuing absolutes, and the result is that tolerance has become a god. Foreclosure seems to push for individuals to accept without question a certain belief system, particularly one that is encouraged by others, an entire community, a society, or a religion. The resulting "group think" becomes the personal belief system. A person needs only to simply agree with what seems to be the current and trendy ideas at the time. The moratorium status has an effect also, more diabolically among people of faith, for if there are trials, troubles, disappointments, and pain, our understanding of people and God are altered dramatically, even to the point of falling away. Finally, achievement is when a person can discern the times, discern the spirits, be able to weather trials and discouragement, all because of unwavering conviction of the truth. Such an individual may declare, as Peter did in John 6:69,

"Lord, to whom shall we go?" [We know, we understand, and we are convinced that], "You have words of eternal life."

These approaches to understanding were true during the time Jesus was born and as He conducted His ministry. For example, Jesus was teaching a new way to understand God, but the disciples kept reverting back to their understanding of the Messiah who was to come. The Jews of that time understood the Messiah was to be a religious leader but more importantly to them, a political leader who would free them from Roman rule and oppression. This is what they had been taught growing up, which was their centuries-long tradition, and they recoiled at the suggestion that their view was off target, even to the point of wanting to kill Jesus. Their "foreclosure" and "group think" prevented them from discerning and embracing the truth which clouded their spiritual understanding. The truth was that Jesus was (and is) the Messiah who freed us from so much more then man's dictatorship....He freed us from the bondage of sin and eternal death.

Judgment vs. Discernment

Perhaps one of the most misunderstood concepts of God is the idea of judgment and how, or if, we are to judge. However, there is a distinction between judgment and condemnation, as there appears to be in the biblical languages as well. It is this distinction that is often misunderstood. The misunderstanding of this concept is so diabolical that Satan has used it towards the tolerance of sin in society and even in the church. Judgment is not to be understood as the opposite of love. This particular misunderstanding can immobilize us, handcuff us, confuse us, and default us into accepting evil.

In our everyday language, we tend to misuse words and interchange words that have different meanings as if they meant the same thing.

For example, we tend to interchange words like house and home; ego and pride; guilt and shame; and affect and effect, just to name a few. While there may be a subtle difference in meaning in these words, the context in which they are used will help determine the meaning, and therefore provide understanding as to what is being said. The misuse of the word can cause misunderstanding and confusion.

This is especially true of the primary biblical languages of Hebrews (Old Testament) and Greek (New Testament). Many words are interchangeable. Also, prefixes may be used in order to enhance or specify a particular meaning. This is true with the words *judgment*, *discernment*, and *condemnation*. While there are specific words for each of these meanings, most of the time, the common words are used interchangeably, and the context renders their meaning. A respected contemporary theologian, F.F. Bruce, who was a professor at the University of Manchester in England, wrote:

> Judgment is an ambiguous word, in English as in Greek: it may mean sitting in judgment on people (or even condemning them), or it may mean exercising a proper discrimination. In the former sense judgment is depreciated; in the latter sense it is recommended (Bruce 1983, 87).

Bruce is using the word, *discrimination*, in the true sense of the word -- to distinguish and separate differences. This is not to advocate what we hear today regarding discrimination, but rather to take heed of what legitimately needs to be set apart, like good and evil.

The Hebrew and Greek languages are among other languages more expressive than English. It is essential to understand that the meaning of words in these languages is determined by the context within which they are used.

As an overview, in the Old Testament, several Hebrew words are used to mean either discernment or judgment, and several are used interchangeably. The most common are as follows:

- *shama* –– to listen; to understand; to diligently consider
- *biyn* –– to separate; to deal wisely with; to direct
- *yada* –– to know; to see; to acknowledge; to understand; to recognize; to discern
- *nakar* –– to scrutinize; become acquainted with; to care about
- *mishpat* –– to render justice; to judge; to give someone either their rights or due punishment;
- *shaphat* –– to judge between; to vindicate; to condemn

The most commonly used Hebrew words are *shaphat* and *mishpat*.

In the New Testament, there are also several Greek words used interchangeably to mean discernment, condemnation, or judgment, as a noun or a verb.

- *krisis* –– judgment; condemnation; damnation; divine judgment
- *krino* –– to differentiate; to rule or govern judicially; to condemn; to punish
- *aisthesis* –– to know; to discover; discernment
- *krima* –– to condemn; to go up against the law; to avenge; damnation
- *kritikos* –– (where we get our word *critical* from) to analyze; separate; differentiate

The most commonly used Greek words are *krino* and *krisis*. Often, the Greek prefix, *dia* is used to indicate the word *discernment*, such as the word *diakrino* and *diakrisis*. (Vine, et al, 1985). Another Greek prefix, *kata*, if applied to a word, like *katakrisis* will mean to "sentence as to condemn." I provide these words to indicate that much of the misunderstanding exists, (a) in the English translation to single words for discernment and judgment, and (b) in the context that these certain words are used.

In the Old Testament, particularly in Exodus 18:13, 15–16, the Hebrew word, *shephat* originally referred to a person who pronounced an oracle –– in other words, one who spoke for God (Harrison, et, al, 1982). Such a person acted like a magistrate or a judge in disputes and conflicts. Later, the use of the word expanded into meaning elders who were appointed to take care of many cases where counsel was needed, in the context of governing. The biblical book, Judges, describes a time when the people of Israel where guided by judges and not monarchs. The similar word, *shaphat* is the verb meaning "to judge, as if to govern" and "to deal wisely with" or "to separate." At times, the word also meant, "to condemn" but in the context of legal judgements.

Discernment has the same meaning, which is to examine, to scrutinize, and the act of separating between things like right and wrong, light and darkness, and good and evil. Spiritual discernment is the grace to see into the unseen. It is a gift of the Spirit to perceive the realm of the spirit. Its purpose is to understand the nature of that which is veiled (Frangipane 2013). Essentially, discernment is seeing clearly. Ezekiel 44:23–24 is a passage that uses two distinct Hebrew words:

> Moreover, they shall teach my people the difference between the holy and the profane, and cause them to discern (*yada*) between the unclean and the clean. And in a dispute they shall take their stand to judge (*shaphat*); they shall judge it according to My ordinances. They shall also keep My laws and My statutes in all my appointed feasts, and sanctify My sabbaths.

God was speaking in this context specifically to the Levites, the priests, whose responsibility was to teach the ways of God and empower the people to make right choices. While we have priests and pastors who have a similar ministry today, the New Testament clearly says that Jesus is our ultimate High Priest (Heb. 4:14–15, 9:11) who *is* God's righteousness and only through Him can we be God's righteousness as well.

There were times that the "congregation" instead of the elders, was given the ability and right to judge situations (Num. 35:24). It was clear and imperative in biblical history that the people of Israel were to be vigilant in their faithfulness to God. In order to remain so, they needed to discern and make judgments resulting in decisions of determining right and wrong or faithfulness and unfaithfulness. Joshua's famous statement is one of many examples of God's directive to His people:

> Now therefore, fear the Lord and serve Him in sincerity and truth; and put away the gods which your fathers served . . . choose for yourselves today whom you will serve . . . but as for me and my house, we will serve the Lord (Joshua 24:14–15).

A case in point is a situation that was recorded in I Corinthians 5:1–5. Paul is writing to the church in Corinth after he was told of an immoral situation among them. Keep in mind his response is *to* the church for a situation *in* the church.

> It is actually reported that there is immorality among you, and immorality of such a kind as does not exist even among the Gentiles, that someone has his father's wife. And you have become arrogant, and have not mourned

instead, in order that the one who had done this deed might be removed from your midst. For I, on my part, though absent in body but present in spirit, have already judged him who has so committed this, as though I were present. In the name of our Lord Jesus, when you are assembled, and I with you in spirit, with the power of our Lord Jesus, deliver such a one to Satan for the destruction of his flesh, that his spirit may be saved in the day of the Lord Jesus (I Cor. 5:1--5).

This passage reveals a situation that leads to a difficult, and seemingly harsh, decision. Paul, who is recognized as a respected apostle and teacher of the Word of God, renders a judgment towards a brother who is living immorally among believers -- having sex with his father's wife. Notice Paul's motivation regarding this person -- "that his spirit may be saved in the day of the Lord Jesus." He had no condemning attitude towards the man, but rather an act of discipline with a bigger picture in mind. Paul clarifies his motivation in another of his writings: "But if we judged ourselves rightly, we should not be judged. But when we are judged, we are disciplined by the Lord in order that we may not be condemned along with the world" (I Cor. 11:31--32).

This is true of parents, law enforcement, and others in authority who desire to see behaviors change in people who are missing the mark. The judgments that parents make, for example, are for disciplinary reasons and based upon loving their child enough to not want them behave a certain way that would lead to trouble and harm. Discipline, when delivered properly, is actually motivated by love, not by hate. Hebrews 12:6--11 states:

For those whom the Lord loves, He disciplines . . . It is for discipline that you endure; God deals with you as with sons; for what son is there whom his father does not discipline? But if you are without discipline, of which all have become partakers, then you are illegitimate children and not sons. Furthermore, we had earthly fathers to discipline us, and we respected them; shall we not much rather be subject to the Father of our spirits, and live? For they disciplined us for a short time as seemed best to them, but He disciplines us for our good, that we may share His holiness. All discipline for the moment seems not to be joyful, but sorrowful; yet to those who have been trained by it, afterwards it yields the peaceful fruit of righteousness.

Clearly, in order to make good decisions, a process of thought evaluation and discernment is required. Judgments have to be made, even about the types of behavior and types of people with whom to associate. In fact, every decision we make is based upon a judgment of some kind. We make highway judgments based on traffic reports, which route to take. We make judgments about what to wear, based upon weather, the type of work we do, or the nature of a particular function we are about to attend. We make dining judgments based upon price, location, and reputation of a specific restaurant. We make judgments as to the friends we make and who we date. When judgment is not made, it is easy to be deceived and be led astray. When we do not honor our "red flags" and concerns, our decisions lead to trouble and negative consequences.

I have counseled with many men and women who ignored their "red flags" and went against their own judgment and made bad decisions, especially as it related to relationships. We all have an innate ability to discern, but we often ignore it. A case in point: actress Lauren Weedman gave an interview for Lindsey Putnam of the *New*

York Post, about how she ignored her discernment. She wanted to hire a babysitter, but the eighteen-year-old babysitter was a very attractive woman, and she had concerns. Her husband eventually developed an affair with the babysitter and as a result, it ruined their marriage:

> But I should have followed my instincts. Other parents warned me about Simone, but as a feminist who works with at-risk girls, I didn't want to pass on a new babysitter just because she was overly sexual. I thought she was just a lost, damaged kid. I thought if I didn't hire her, it would make me look like some old insecure troll. I was trying to prove to David that I was cool. If I didn't feel comfortable, I should have just said so, and not cared what anyone else thought (Putnam, 2016).

Our personal, biases, agendas, assumptions, and fears often cloud our ability to see clearly. Seeing clearly, understanding what we are seeing, and making judgments accordingly is essential. Honoring our discernment is not judging – it is wise. It can help prevent many unwanted consequences.

The spiritual gift of discernment of spirits (1Cor. 12:10) is perhaps not utilized enough –- notice it is a gift to be used! Doctrinal traditions that believe the spiritual gifts are not for the modern church are hampering believers from using what is available to them through the Holy Spirit. I believe that becomes detrimental to living a full Christian life, if we do not employ that which God has provided for us.

On the other hand, some people believe *they* can make someone else a better person, or that in a different situation, *they* can change another person. Never take on that mission –- such a mindset sets you up for failure. If you seek to change something about another person then pay attention to that desire for it indicates that you dislike, or even hate, something about them in the first place. The truth is no one has the power to change another person –– the changing force in all our lives is the Holy Spirit –– if we allow Him to do so. To expect anything different sets us up for heartache and disappointment.

For example, to begin a relationship with a known addict is not a good idea. Making such a judgment is for your own wellbeing. An addiction to pornography, sex, drugs, alcohol, gambling, or spending has the great potential of eventually destroying a person, and the people around them. Someone who is in bondage to an addiction will often do anything –– and I mean anything –– to get their fix, even at the expense of those they love. It has been estimated that for every addict, at least five people are affected. You don't have to be one of them.

As a counselor, my experience is that addicts are typically connivers, liars, defensive, manipulators, and sometimes abusive. If you are with someone who is abusive, you often feel shut down and trapped. The abusive person can be "gas-lighting" you, which is the manipulative act of attempting to change your memory or perception of events in *their* favor, making you feel crazy or like you have forgotten something. Such mind game tactics to always make you feel you are wrong, alters your ability to understand the situation and to see clearly. The manipulated person needs to make a judgment to get away, and receive help in establishing clarity of mind and emotions, in order to make better decisions towards safety.

One individual I was counseling whose wife and two children left him due to his drinking, and related unhealthy behaviors, made a statement that could not have been more profound and descriptive. He said, "I was selfish and numb." His only motivation was for himself and to meet his own needs. To avoid getting into a relationship with someone who exhibits those tendencies is good judgment. Judging in this manner is not evil. The addict needs to change, but he or she needs to admit the need to change. Addicts need to be convinced to the point that it changes their lives by acknowledging they have a weakness and a need to surrender to God. Too often, rehab centers address only the addiction itself, but what is needed is getting to the root of what drives the addiction in the first place.

To help people, whether one is a doctor, counselor, minister, law enforcement officer, or first responder, discernment is essential, as it leads to making value judgments in situations. Discernment and judgment are critical in military operations as well as it could be a matter of life and death. Making judgments to rectify situations in individuals' lives is not judging them –- it is helping them, and perhaps those around them. "At times we may have to intervene to stop destructive behavior. For example, when some members of a family confront another who is an alcoholic because he is destroying himself and his relationship with them, this is loving" (Boyd 2004, 187).

As my father was immersed in alcoholism, I can remember many times his doctor telling him that he needed to stop drinking and get help or it would kill him. The doctor also told him to stop smoking for the same reason. Was the doctor judging my father? I never felt that way. Nor did I ever hear my dad say, "Stop judging me." The doctor was making judgments about his destructive behaviors in the spirit of caring for him. However, the doctor could not force his patient to change his life. If people refuse to adhere to wisdom, sometimes the approach is to leave them to themselves. Jesus taught:

> And if your brother sins, go and reprove him in private; if
> he listens to you, you have won your brother. But if he does

not listen to you, take one or two more with you, so that by the mouth of two or three witnesses every fact may be confirmed. And if he refuses to listen to them, tell it to the church; and if he refuses to listen even to the church, let him be to you as a Gentile and a tax-gatherer (Matt. 18:15—17).

When police officers come upon a suspicious person or situation, they are trained and have every right to make a judgment toward action, if they believe a threatening act is about to occur, a law is being broken, or the public is in danger. The vast majority of the time, the officer is correct in discerning the action he needs to take. If we have never been a police officer, we cannot understand what it is like to have to make a split-second decision, in a life and death situation. Without the ability to make a judgment, many people could be at risk. To "judge not" would be a mistake. "It is impossible to make an ethical judgment without passing judgment upon the one who performs the act" (Harrison, et al 1982, 303).

There are times when we need to adjust the way we think and act. There are also appropriate times when someone needs to confront us and suggest to us alternative considerations. Suggesting corrective ways of living is an act of caring. Parents have the right to correct their children, and most do so with love as a motivation.

Correction is not the same as criticism. What people react to is the false assumption that criticism and condemnation are being rendered. Correction says, "This is why you are where you are, and I care enough about you to see better outcomes in your life." Condemnation says, "You are horrible; stupid; useless; etc., and you will never change —- there is no hope for you."

I have been around many people who, when caught doing something wrong, or simply falling short of expectations, would say, "Don't judge me." What they are really saying is, "I know I am doing something wrong, but I don't want to hear about it." Or they may be saying, "Whatever you say will add to my self-condemnation, and I can't take any more of that." They may not want correction, perhaps because they haven't felt someone who cared enough, and because correction is equated with criticism. What is also being said, although it is much more diabolical and subtle, is there are no absolutes or there is no hope. Instead, it is believed that the only absolutes are those that make us happy. Anything that does not make us happy is seen as intrusive, insulting, cramping our style, offensive, and irrelevant. As a result, God or anyone in a position of authority is seen as a killjoy or an abuser.

For millennials in particular (individuals born in the years ranging from the early 1980s to the early 2000s), it's all about personal circumstances, according to Robert Jones, CEO of Public Religion Research Institute (PRRI) (Grossman 2015). For the millennials, it is all about situational ethics and empathy, according to Jones. He conducted a survey of 2,314 millennials in the United States from February 12 –-15, 2015. Some of his findings are as follows:

- Most young adults hold views on moral issues that are a long way from what some major religions preach.
- 56 percent of millennials say that in some situations, choosing to have an abortion "is the most responsible decision that a woman can make."
- Millennials seem reluctant to make blanket black-and-white moral pronouncements about issues they see as complex.
- Majorities of black Protestants, white mainline Protestants and white Catholics all say abortion should be legal in all or most cases –- in contrast to 80 percent of white evangelical

millennials who believe abortion should be illegal in all or most cases.

- One-quarter of millennials say that marriage has become old-fashioned and out of date (Grossman 2015).

However, the usual emphasis on what it means to judge, to make someone feel condemned, has rendered us ineffective in eradicating evil and ineffective in helping someone make better decisions. As a result, families and even entire communities have been negatively affected by allowing rebellion and evil. Better decisions come from a transformed heart and a desire to *follow* Jesus, not just believe in Him. Jesus Himself often made it clear that certain behaviors, statements, and lifestyles were against God's ways (Matt 16:23, John 6:30). He also lovingly invited many to follow Him as the way to attain a new life, peace, and contentment (John 10:9–10; John 11:25–26). "God doesn't judge us based on the worst decision we make in life, but on the best decision we make in life. And that is to let Jesus save us" (Weece 2016, 90).

So, how can we understand such an emotional concept? Can we return to the ability to make better judgments in the face of evil, even if it means to do so would challenge a person's behavior? Can we develop the right motivation behind judgments so that a person may understand we have the greater good in mind? These are questions that need to be answered in order to correct the lawless tendencies that have increasingly developed around us. Allow me to provide just a few examples of this important concept.

Everyone seems to know certain quotes of Jesus that are brandished about for their own purposes. For example, we hear, "Love your neighbor as yourself" (which is the basis of what we call the "Golden Rule"). We also hear, "What goes around comes around" (although Jesus never said that; Paul declares what a sower sows will be what he reaps in Gal. 6:7–8). We often hear people quote Jesus, "Do not judge lest you be judged" (Matt. 7:1). The context here is important.

The Greek word in Matthew 7:1 is *krino*, and is often translated "condemn." We can legitimately read this statement as, "Do not condemn lest you be condemned." However, the context in which Jesus was speaking "shows that what Jesus had in mind was that one must not judge another without first judging oneself. A Christian judgment should reflect the mind of Christ and should begin with an examination of self" (Harrison, 1983, 303). Jesus was addressing the human tendency to be too quick to judge another without looking at oneself first. He used the word picture of taking the log out of our eye before we attempted to remove the speck from another person's eye (Matt 7:3–5). The apostle Paul addresses the same tendency, when he states in Romans 2:3, "And do you suppose this, O man, when you pass judgment upon those who practice such things and do the same yourself, that you will escape the judgment of God?" What we all are guilty of is noticing another's shortcoming, at the same time as we overlook our own. This is what Jesus' was warning us against.

Once we address our own issues, then we can more lovingly and effectively address another person's issues. Jesus is after the *spirit* of confrontation. Confrontation that communicates sincere concern for someone's choices and wellbeing will invite the other person to consider their ways. Consider the model of Alcoholics Anonymous (AA) or Teen Challenge. The participants in these groups are themselves recovering from alcohol or drug addiction, and when they challenge their fellow members, it is coming from an "I have been there, and I know it does not work" attitude. They are in the process of, or have already, taken the log out of their own eye and can legitimately address the speck in another's eye.

Many counselors, social workers, pastors, and other professional care givers are in these professions because of what they overcame and the desire to give back to others to help them do the same. It is this spirit that Jesus was encouraging people to have. First examine yourself, acknowledge your "log," be willing to honestly deal with it, and begin to overcome it, before you address someone else in similar situations.

The eye is the most tender, most sensitive part of the human body. How do you take a speck out of someone's eye? Very carefully! First, you must gain his or her trust. This means consistently demonstrating an attitude that does not instinctively condemn. Condemnation separates. "The judgment Jesus prohibits is not about ascribing worth to others by helping them be free from things in their lives that suppress their worth. It's about trying to experience worth *for oneself* by *detracting* it from others" (Boyd 2004, 107). To help others, we must first see clearly (Frangipane 2013). However, if the spirit is one of condemnation and self-righteousness, the resulting contentiousness leads to separation, rejection, and conflict.

Essentially, in many cases we have to "earn" the right to correct someone by approaching with care and humility with the well-being of the other in mind. Galatians 6:1 states, "Brethren, even if a man is caught in any trespass, you who are spiritual, restore such a one in a spirit of gentleness; each one looking to yourself, lest you too be tempted." Without the attitudes of humility, gentleness, and correction with the other person's wellbeing in mind, we will repel people, not restore them. Going in with the intent of love and care will be more fruitful. Otherwise it would feel like using a sledge hammer to kill an ant.

In Luke 6:37 we read Jesus declare, "And do not judge and you will not be judged; and do not condemn, and you will not be condemned; pardon, and you will be pardoned." Here two different words are used –– *krino* for judge and *katadikazo* for condemned. When the context is considered, especially with the word *pardoned*, the word *krino* is better understood here as "avenge" or also "condemn." When someone is already condemned, the antidote, if you will, is to be pardoned. We will reap what we sow (Gal. 6:7––8), and Jesus was simply making the case to be careful how we render judgment, for whatever we do will come to back to us. The broader context in this chapter is Jesus speaking about love, mercy, and generosity.

Condemnation can refer either to the legal status of liability to punishment or to the actual infliction of that punishment. This legal process is to some extent the background for biblical language about judgment and condemnation. What we believe about Jesus places us in either a place of condemnation or of pardon. For example, Jesus said, "And this is the judgment that the light is come into the world, and men loved the darkness rather than the light; for their deeds were evil" (John 3:19). Also, Jesus stated, "Truly, truly, I say to you, he who hears my word and believes Him who sent Me, has eternal life and does not come into judgment, but has passed out of death into life" (John 5:24). In both these cases, the meaning is "condemnation" because of context, and the Greek word used is *krisis*.

There is good news about condemnation. Jesus made a way to reverse it, as Roman 8:1 declares, "There is now no condemnation for those who are in Christ Jesus." Only in Christ can we be pardoned. We either condemn ourselves by our unbelief and rejection of Christ, thereby living under the unforgivable sin, or we can accept Jesus and be pardoned and given new life. Only God can condemn and only God can pardon and declare innocence. Condemnation is not the judging in which believers participate.

Another example to consider is found in John 3:17 where Jesus says, "For God did not send the Son into the world to judge the world but that the world should be saved through Him." The word *judge* here is once again, *krino*, and again it is better understood to mean condemn or punish. The very next verse adds understanding: "He who believes in Him is not judged (*krino*); he who does not believe has been judged already, because he has not believed in the name of the only begotten Son of God" (v. 18). Jesus is referring to condemnation because of rejection of Christ. Of course the well-known verse John 3:16 comes a couple of verses before, and in context, Jesus was referring to Himself as being the ultimate antidote to condemnation and His first coming to earth. His mission was to provide a loving, God-endorsed, drastic, sacrificial atonement for sin and death. His first coming was to focus on restoring the way to the Father by overcoming sin, condemnation, and death. In the future, when Jesus comes again, His ministry will be entirely different -- He will judge (*separate to life or condemnation* His sheep from the goats for eternity) (2 Thess. 1:6--8; John 5:22--24).

Finally, James 4:10--12 says:

Humble yourselves in the presence of the Lord, and He will exalt you. Do not speak against one another, brethren. He who speaks against a brother, or judges his brother, speaks against the law, and judges the law; but if you judge the law, you are not doer of the law, but a judge of it. There is only one Lawgiver and Judge, the One who is able to save and destroy; but who are you to judge your neighbor . . . But as it is, you boast in your arrogance; all such boasting is evil. Therefore, the one who knows the right thing to do, and does not do it, to him it is sin.

Keep in mind that the Bible consistently teaches the law

condemns, because no one can completely live the Law by their own power, thereby all falling short of the ideal. In this context, James is discussing things to avoid as believers. Speaking against (*katalaleo*) one another means literally to slander, lie, or demean another, especially a Christian brother or sister, which clearly goes against Christian love and edification. James repeats Jesus's teaching of being humble, and being sure *we* do what *we* know to be right first.

James then shows us that by taking the law into our own hands, we are essentially making the law fit our views, and only God is the Lawgiver and ultimate Judge. The Greek word here for judge is once again, *krino*, and in this context the connotation is "condemn."

Ultimately, no one has the power to condemn except God. Condemnation is a final state of no return, communicating no hope. At times the word is also used to refer to negative evaluations of a person by others or by one's own conscience –- in other words, self-condemnation. It is the feeling of self-condemnation that often leads to depression, despair, hopelessness, and even suicide. First John 3:21 says, "Beloved, if our heart does not condemn us, we have confidence before God." The constant wave of bullying, face-to-face or through cyber-bullying, can cause a person to develop a feeling of condemnation. We have heard of many occasions where a young person completes suicide as a result of constant bullying and condemnation. When people feel useless, unloved, not valued, or a constant failure, they may sink into depression, feelings of condemnation, and a sense of hopelessness.

Paul writes in 2 Corinthians 7:1–-3:

Therefore, having these promises, beloved, let us cleanse ourselves from all defilement of flesh and spirit, perfecting holiness in the fear of God. Make room for us in your hearts; we wronged no one, we corrupted no one, we took advantage of no one. I do not speak to condemn you; for I have said before that you are in our hearts to die together and to live together.

Clearly, the apostle is encouraging his listeners toward holiness, but is not condemning them in doing so. He makes it clear that he has had a relationship with them, as they have been in his heart, so he feels free to admonish them. Incidentally, the Greek word used here is, *katakrisis*, and is rendered *condemned* because of the prefix and the context.

Then we read in 1Corinthians 6:2--3, 5:

Or do you not know that the saints will judge the world? And if the world is judged by you, are you not competent to constitute the smallest law courts? Do you not know that we shall judge angels? How much more, matters in this life? . . . Is it so, that there is not among you one wise man who will be able to decide between his brethren . . .?

At first, we read what appears to be a contradiction from what Jesus stated. So, which is it? Jesus and Paul seem to be at odds with each other over this concept, right? This is a great example of the context determining the meaning of the same word. The word used here is once again the Greek word, *krino*. To "decide between his brethren" is a mandate and a privilege. Here we understand the word to mean, to distinguish, and then make a judgment accordingly. As Christians, we have the ability to declare good from evil and light from darkness. To make such distinctions is essential for good decision making and walking in righteousness. To make such distinctions is not condemnation. The legitimate process should be as follows:

- Recognize the issue and its current or potential consequences
- Consider it as either good or evil, according to God's Word
- Distinguish or separate accordingly
- Pray and seek God's wisdom
- Then make a judgment or decision

There is nothing wrong with this process. We all actually use this process in everything we do as we make decisions, whether the decisions are small and mundane or huge and critical. However, as Jesus taught, this process is to be applied to each of us first, before it can be applied to another.

However, there is a challenge today. The more evil, rebellion, and resistance to the light of the gospel increases, the less individuals and the culture want to be corrected. Increasingly, there is a love for the things in darkness and contempt for the things in the light. Chesterton said, "Fallacies do not cease to be fallacies because they become fashions" (Belmonte 2011, 64). Lawlessness has become accepted over and above being arrested for breaking the law. Sexual lifestyles have become accepted, making the *declaration* of their immorality more evil than the behaviors themselves. It is these times we may hear, "Do not judge lest you be judged." However, Proverbs 28:5 states, "Evil men understand not judgment (*mishpat*; justice); but they that seek the Lord understand all things" (KJV, emphasis mine).

We are living in a time when a growing number of people do not want to acknowledge evil and rebellion, and those who seek to bring righteousness into a situation are the ones who are vilified. Those who walk in rebellion, pride, and arrogance are claiming to be judged, when in reality they are being convicted and are unwilling to positively respond to conviction. Conviction can either direct us back to God, or it can repel us away from God. The first direction leads to repentance and restoration to God. The second direction leads to shame, self-justification, and further separation from God and one another, and ultimately condemnation. The ones who call out evil are considered to be the problem today, rather than those who are in need of correction or have broken the law. We have accepted tolerance as a virtue in too many things, and as a result, we have seen an increase in lawlessness.

History has provided countless examples of what occurs when good people do nothing. For example, when parts of the world "tolerated" Adolf Hitler, the leader of Nazi Germany from 1933 to 1945, and chose to go along and appease him, it turned out to be a costly mistake and much of the world suffered as a result. It is more prudent and indeed more appropriate to not tolerate evil, immorality, and lawlessness despite what others may say. Corrupt government, arrogant agendas, immoral assertions, and imbalanced legislation are to be challenged, not tolerated. Because we are accepting more deviant ways of thinking and behaviors, all in the name of tolerance, we are increasingly experiencing confusion, chaos, immorality, and lawlessness. In these cases, making judgment is necessary. The call we may hear is that of discrimination and prejudice. However, it is protective and necessary to discriminate between good and evil, light and darkness, arrogance and prudence, and pride and humility –– regardless of one's ethnicity. We will never go wrong in doing so as long as the Spirit of God and God's Word are the standards.

Yet our mission is to remember to evaluate ourselves first and seek transformation in our lives through Jesus. It is also important to seek understanding of another person's situation, before rendering judgment. Our mission is to carry out Jesus's mission –– to speak truth yet to see people and situations through the eyes of redemption, not condemnation. Consider Galatians 6:1–3:

> Brethren, even if a man is caught in any trespass, you who are spiritual, restore such a one in a spirit of gentleness; each one looking to yourself, lest you too be tempted. Bear one another's burdens, and thus fulfill the law of Christ. For if anyone thinks he is something when he is nothing, he deceives himself.

The apostle Paul makes it clear that the intent of confrontation and making judgment between right and wrong in a person's life is that of restoration. Like Jesus, Paul makes clear to be sure we look at ourselves first. In doing so, we can approach another person with a spirit of gentleness because we have known from what we have been restored in our own lives. The gratefulness and humility that occurs when we see how Jesus forgave and restored us, can be expressed when we confront another.

When Jesus and His disciples were scorned and rejected by some in Samaria, the disciples asked, "Lord, do you want us to command fire to come down from heaven and consume them? (Luke 9:54). Jesus responded with, "You do not know what kind of spirit you are of" (Luke 9:55). As we grow in *His* righteousness and humility, we may have the privilege to confront someone about his or her life. Doing so in the spirit of correction and not criticism is critical. "And if your brother sins, go and reprove him in private; if he listens to you, you have won your brother" (Matt.18:15). "The judgment Jesus prohibits is not about distinguishing between good and bad behaviors or between life in union with God versus life in separation from God — it is about *separating people*" (Boyd 2004, 107). The goal is to win your brother or sister, gain his or her trust, and encourage genuine change. To keep their well-being and betterment in mind will bring more openness than rejection.

In order for us to be effective in discerning and making sound judgments, we have to remain faithful to what we know to be pleasing to God. Then and only then can we think about confronting others. The spirit in which we do so will determine the level of impacting for good the person with whom we are in relationship. Ephesians 5:11–13 states:

> And do not participate in the unfruitful deeds of darkness, but instead even expose them; for it is disgraceful even to speak of the things which are done by them in secret. But all things become visible when they are exposed by the light, for everything that becomes visible is light.

Our goal is not to show others what we know and how to change them. It is an honor and a privilege to help another person separate good from evil and light and darkness from his or her life. But we have to earn that right based upon the level of relationship we have with others and the spirit in which we approach them. If done correctly and with the right attitude and spirit, understanding will take place. James 2:13 says, "Mercy triumphs over judgment," (*krisis*, condemnation). Correct understanding can then lead to positive change and better decision making and actions for us and others alike.

We can only give that which we have, so if we walk in self-condemnation, we will dish out condemnation to others. If we believe that we have to perform in order to be accepted, then we will impose that same belief onto others. There are Christians I know who have not made spiritual progress for years. They attend church and they tithe, yet they maintain a self-righteous, condemning attitude. They always have something negative to say about others. As such, they position themselves under God's judgment. Romans 2:3 states, "And do you suppose this, O man, when you pass judgment [*krima* = *condemnation*] upon those who practice such things and do the same yourself, that you will escape the judgment [*krima*] of God?" The capacity to receive divine mercy is closed because a person does not show mercy toward others. Understand that you are pardoned and redeemed from the burden of falling short. When we can walk in freedom, we can confront others with the same hope.

John 8:1–11 records the scene when a woman was caught in the very act of adultery by some Pharisees (I wonder how *they* knew where to find her?), and these religious leaders brought her to Jesus. They demanded that He accuse and condemn her, but secretly they had another reason for bringing her before Jesus. They wanted to accuse and judge Him! According to the Law, she was worthy of being stoned to death (Lev. 20:10; Deut. 22:22). Instead, Jesus turned the condemning tables onto the crowd, among whom the Pharisees stood. Jesus invited anyone who was without sin to cast the first stone. Instead, one by one, the men in the crowd dispersed, leaving the woman alone with Jesus (John 8:7–9). The issue was condemnation, and there was no one left to render a final judgment on the woman. With that, Jesus said, "Neither do I condemn you; go your way. From now on sin no more" (John 8:11). We can understand that Jesus expressed grace to the woman, did not condemn her even in her guilt, and directed her to change her lifestyle and no longer commit adultery again. With gracious correction, comes the power to walk in righteousness, if we accept God's grace.

Have you ever heard Christians accuse God of something? I hear it often from people in counseling. For example, "God isn't working in my life" or "I pray faithfully, but He doesn't answer" or "I've done everything I can, but He still hasn't set me free." Satan wants us to accuse God in our hearts. It creates an endless cycle of bondage and discouragement. Notice what Jesus then said to the woman: "Where are they? Has no one condemned (*katakrino*) you?" (8:10). Jesus similarly declares to us today: "Where are your accusers? Where are the voices that say, 'You're sinful, hopeless, a failure?' They're gone!" Jesus is your righteousness now, and He has silenced all condemnation.

Correction is not condemnation. Correction's intent is to adjust a person's thinking and lifestyle out of love and concern. Condemnation's intent is to render a hopeless, final sentence upon someone out of fear and hatred. Jesus showed love and grace, yet He also directed the woman caught in adultery to make some corrections in her life. Both were appropriate and well received by the woman. One without the other leads to an imbalanced response. Too much tolerance and grace leads to continued sin and assumptions that sin is acceptable, and too much correction will feel like criticism and condemnation and will crush our spirits, and we will feel hopeless, with no motivation to change. Jesus spoke of such a balance when He stated, "Behold, I send you forth as sheep in the midst of wolves: be ye therefore wise as serpents, and harmless as doves" (Matt. 10:16, KJV).

To summarize, discernment and judgment are necessary in our daily lives. How we discern and from what foundation, can make the difference. Judging is not evil, hateful judging is. Here are some guidelines:

- Honor your "red flags" –– pay attention to your discernment and concerns. Consider them, don't ignore them, and then make judgment accordingly. That is not condemnation.

- Do not judge based upon rumors or gossip (Lev. 19:16; Prov. 11:13; 16:28).
- Do not misjudge heart, motives, or destinies (1 Sam. 16:1–7).
- Do not judge others for sins *you* have; that's called projecting onto others what is really true of you (Prov. 16:2).
- Do not be quick to judge others –- focus on you first (Matt. 7:1-5)
- Do not judge others for breaking *your* contrived rules (Col. 2:16-23).
- Only judge matters within your own "jurisdiction" or personal responsibility (Matt. 18:15–17). Correction is not condemnation, but you need to earn the ability to correct based on your role and level of relationship.
- Judgment is not the same as condemnation; although we all need to be careful not to condemn, which can be easy to do. Only God can condemn, and He does so based upon a person's ultimate rejection of Christ.
- We will all one day stand before God (Rom. 14:5–13).

The next few chapters will address several things that address the ways we understand or misunderstand ourselves and others.

PART II
Understanding Self and Others

CHAPTER 5

Clarity –– Setting Us Free from Deceptions

Folly is joy to him who lacks sense (heart), but a man of understanding walks straight.

> –– Prov. 15:21

Rarely do we find men who willingly engage in hard, solid thinking. There is an almost universal quest for easy answers and half-baked solutions. Nothing pains some people more than having to think.

> –– Dr. Martin Luther King, Jr.

Lamont was packing for a business trip out of town. As he picked up his toothbrush, he noticed the toothpaste tube was almost finished. He noticed there was a another tube in the other bathroom in the house, so he packed the first tube, thinking he would finish it while away and not have to bring it back home. As he was packing, his wife noticed that the toothpaste was gone from their bathroom, and asked her husband, "Did you just pack the toothpaste from our bathroom?" Lamont acknowledged that he did, and before he could say any more, his wife proclaimed, "That's selfish of you, packing our toothpaste and leaving none in our bathroom!" Lamont was taken aback and felt totally misunderstood. His intentions were practical and harmless, but also misread, and he was just accused of something that only an assumption would produce –– and a wrong one at that.

In my previous book, *Created for Purpose*, I discussed the weapons of Satan. One of his weapons, and the one that perhaps affects understanding the most, is that of deception (doubt can be included at times as well). Deception takes the truth and distorts it, hides it, misconstrues it, and ignores it – all with the effect of creating misunderstandings. For understanding to occur, we need to know the truth. Jesus taught, "The truth shall make you free" (John 8:32). While Jesus was referring to freedom from sin because of the truth of the gospel through Him, it can be said that the truth about anything is liberating. Jesus did not just speak the truth; He is the truth! As we have learned in a previous chapter, the truth is personified in Christ and God's "body language" provides complete understanding of who God is and His message to humankind. However, truth is so powerful that it can set us free from several things, and misunderstanding is one of them.

Deception is a strong weapon that the devil employs to prevent understanding. Deception often appears as filters through which we view the world, ourselves, and God. Some filters are covert hindrances, causing misunderstanding. In other words, they are hidden and we are not often aware of them. We will discuss those in the next chapter.

Then there are overt hindrances, whereby a person makes deliberate choices based upon emotions, misinformation, rebellion, and acts of the will. "The opposite of self-awareness is self-deception. And if the truth can set us free, a lie can hold us hostage" (Weece 2016, 53).

Three primary overt filters of deception are assumptions, perceptions, and intentions. While these concepts are sometimes used interchangeably, they are not the same.

Assumptions

Assumptions can make us look foolish or get us in trouble, (as a common cliché about assuming indicates). Yet, we do it all the time. Assumptions more often than not determine what we believe, how we feel, and how we act. While we are often too slow to observe and consider "red flags," assumptions are when we are too quick to make judgments. "Jesus is inviting us to trade our instinctive responses for reflective responses" (Weece 2016, 79). We are usually unaware of the assumptions we hold onto. "The amazing thing is, the 'assumption' part of our decision-making process is usually the part that gets the least examination" (Overman 1996, 16).

Assumptions are thought processes that are typically impacted by twisted biases, incorrect stereotypes, various rumors, emotional responses, and cultural prejudices. Stated simply, assumptions are mostly flawed. Assumptions are often devoid of facts, truths, and discernment, centered on personal agendas. Our agendas essentially dictate what we want life to look like, and what we want ourselves to look like. Even so-called research and academic investigation are often biased in the direction of the assumption to the point that we refuse to see anything else that may contradict our assumptions. In our minds, assumptions eventually become strong opinion and then fact. Basically, we assume that we're no longer assuming (Lounsbrough, 2015).

Assumptions can have a detrimental effect upon our understanding of situations and people. "The problem with making assumptions is that we *believe* that they are the truth" (Ruiz, 1997, 63). As a result, assumptions are often so ingrained, that they may be difficult to change. When assumptions do change, it is usually through difficult circumstances that no longer feed our chosen assumptions. "What's more, we continue to live and act in certain ways until such time we become convinced our assumptions are in need of change" (Overman 1996, 17). Case in point:

> In 2004, President George W. Bush had an encounter with recording artist Elton John. The men were on opposite sides of the political spectrum. "I wasn't a big fan of his policies," John said. "His policies didn't sit well with mine." But not long after Bush launched his anti- AIDS effort, John had a chance to meet him. The occasion was the 2004 Kennedy Center honors. "At the Kennedy Center concert we spent some time in the intermission with the president, George Bush, and he was amazingly informed about AIDS," John recounted. "He treated us with such kindness. I had so much respect for him, especially when the PEPFAR [President's Emergency Plan for AIDS Relief] thing was announced when he gave 15 billion dollars to AIDS. He knew what he was talking about." Personal interaction caused John to change his view of Bush. "One of the old adages in life is never judge someone until you meet them," John said. "I didn't like his policies, but I have to say when I met him, I found him charming, I found him well informed, and I found him determined to do something about the AIDS situation, so I changed my opinion of him. And his wife was astonishingly kind to us as well. So it was—I learned a lesson" (Karl, Coolidge, and Pham 2012).

A lesson learned indeed. We make assumptions based upon

"group think" and hearsay, which often are inaccurate and filled with agendas. When we have preconceived, emotionally-driven ideas and don't understand something, we often make assumptions.

When we have legitimized our agendas by converting our assumptions to fact, we can become quite dangerous. Turek states, "Lies are born the moment someone thinks the truth is dangerous" (Turek 2016). We are not likely to question our agendas because they have "facts," and in doing so we would be forced to waste all of our efforts and energy that have helped us arrive at such "facts." In other words, whatever you believe to be true, you do. We would also be forced to face the world as it is, rather than perpetuate the world that we've worked too hard to fabricate (Lounsbrough, 2015).

We would also have to see ourselves in the true light, which human nature tries to avoid at all costs. As a result, we are forced to create a world that we are not living in, to become people that we're not, to make other people out to be what they are not, to see situations as something other than what they truly are, and to miss the truth of life through the entire process of fabricating life by the application of our assumptions (Lounsbrough, 2015). All of which clouds the ability to truly understand something or someone.

It is essential that we all change from the practice of forming facts from assumptions and agendas. Lounsbrough (2015) suggests several things to do. First, we need to be reflectively honest with ourselves. This is costly because it may mean that we admit we are protecting ourselves from the real world by being something that we are not, and believing something that is false. However, the reward is arriving at the knowledge of the truth that can indeed bring peace. There is a saying that is full of truth: "Confession is good for the soul." Psalm 32:2 says, "How blessed is the man . . . in whose spirit there is no deceit!" Psalm 119 provides many promises to those who are open, honest, contrite, and seek forgiveness.

Second, we must begin to believe that while the real world is in need of true change, and not covered over with our deceiving assumptions, we have to do the changing first (Lounsbrough 2015). I have found that when a person first considers marriage, he or she often has a mission to change the other person. When people desire to change someone else to conform to what they want, the mission will always fail. "If we try to change them, this means we don't really like them" (Ruiz 1997, 70). The first mission should be to seek to change you. One of the positive mysteries of marriage is that once we make sincere and lasting changes, we find that our spouse begins to change as well, but *in response to* our new outlook, attitudes, and behaviors. But the truth is, "If others change, it's because they want to change, not because you can change them" (Ruiz 1997, 70).

While the world is a tough place, it is also a hurting place (Lounsbrough 2015). It really makes no sense to make a hurting world worse by our assumptions. "We make an assumption, we misunderstand, we take it personally, and we end up creating a whole big drama for nothing" (Ruiz 1997, 64). We are called to help the hurting, but that often requires that we extinguish the troubled situation first before help can be offered. The duality is often difficult to understand. Changing our life does not mean we create something that is not. Rather, to change means that we seek a new mind, heart, and set of eyes, in order to see ourselves as we are, and the world as it is. Then perhaps, we can be effective in helping others.

Next, we need to abandon all assumptions, despite how comforting and convenient they tend to be (Lounsbrough 2015). The power to do so lies in the understanding that the inherently flawed nature of assumptions will always do more harm than good. "It is always better to ask questions than to make an assumption, because assumptions set us up for suffering" (Ruiz 1997, 65). For example, we often make the mistake of assuming that our spouse knows what we think and that we do not have to ask for what we want. When we become disappointed, we will feel hurt and angry and say something like, "You should have known." Conflict is sure to arise from the frustration of moments like this. The solution is to seek clarification. One of my life slogans is, "It doesn't hurt to ask." It takes courage to ask questions. It takes effort too. If you don't understand, ask. More often than not, we would rather take the lazy road and simply assume. Not a good idea.

Because our tendency is to be in the know, as mentioned in an earlier chapter, we want an answer to fill the void, and so we may make one up. "There are so many things that the reasoning mind cannot explain. It is not important if the answer is correct; just the answer itself makes us feel safe. This is why we make assumptions" (Ruiz 1997, 68). We long for understanding so strongly that we often depend on our power to "fill in the blank." It does not feel safe to be in the land of the unknown. But it is better than assuming something that is false and often hurtful. Our need to know can simply be satisfied by a dialog and asking questions and clarifying.

Fourth, we must develop agendas not based solely on our agendas (Lounsbrough 2015). What does God want? What would Jesus do? How can we truly help someone? As a counseling and ministry educator, I come across student interns who believe they must "fix" others or "fix" their client's circumstances. The intern counselor or minister may feel pressure that it is up to them to change another person or the circumstances, as if the credibility of their ministry rests upon their efforts. We need to understand that the effort to change actually rests in the one receiving ministry. Undoubtedly,

God will use us, but ultimately, it is the power of God that does the healing and changing in an individual, but are we asking for it and believing in what is necessary? Look how often in Jesus' ministry He required something from someone He chose to heal. The essential requirement was faith in Jesus and His word. For example:

- A woman, because of her faith, reached out and touched Jesus' garment and she was healed (Matt. 9:21–22).
- Someone had to fill the pots with water, as Jesus instructed, before the water was turned into wine at the wedding in Cana (John 2:7–9).
- In Bethesda, Jesus healed a crippled man by first asking, "Do you wish to get well?" and upon the man's affirmation Jesus declared, "Take up you pallet and walk" and the man was healed (John 5:5–9). Then, Jesus told the man to go and sin no more, ". . . so that nothing worse may befall you" (v. 14), implying that his condition was at least partially caused by his choices.
- Ten lepers were healed after Jesus said to them, "Go and show yourselves to the priests" and as they went they were healed (Luke 17:11–19).
- A man born blind, had to go wash off the mud Jesus placed on his eyes, after which he was healed and gained his sight (John9:6–7).

Finally, we must not let the assumptions of others become our assumptions (Lounsbrough 2015). The "group think" dynamic can be powerful and influential, but we need to be willing to accept rejection if we do not adopt someone else's assumptions. G. K. Chesterton stated, "Public opinion can be a prairie fire. It eats up everything that opposes it" (Belmonte 2011, 220). Group assumptions have the power to present what appears to be true since after all, so many people can't be wrong, right?

Political and religious thinking are sometimes developed from a "group think" mentality. Protest mobs are often guilty of this. Many people feel intimidated into believing something for fear of rejection, retribution, or even harm. Dangerous decisions are made simply because so many people may believe a lie. To understand the truth clearly, we must be careful about the things that we accept as truth. We must be ever mindful of the "convenience" of believing what everyone else believes and instead courageously be willing to search for the truth.

The biblical figure Nicodemus is a case in point. He sought out Jesus. He was a Pharisee, a group of religious leaders and teachers in Israel at the time who wanted to silence and kill Jesus. These leaders assumed a great deal about Jesus based on some false accusations, and as a result, their understanding was skewed. They also misinterpreted the scriptures. However, Nicodemus apparently did not succumb to group think. He came out during the night because he may have been embarrassed, and feared ridicule, but he searched for the truth by encountering Jesus personally (John 3:1--21). Imagine someone today attempting to think differently than the group with which they identify. It takes courage and a desire for understanding. In fact, to understand and seek truth takes courage. Whether it is a political group, an ethnic group, or a religious group, a person who considers something other than a group think assumption is a truth seeker, but is also subject to name calling and ostracization.

Nicodemus posed several questions, and Jesus answered each one. Yet, he still had difficulty understanding. Then Jesus provided an alternative to assumptions by introducing the concept of convictions:

> Are you the teacher of Israel, and do not understand these things? Truly, truly I say to you, we speak that which we know, and bear witness of that which we have seen; and you do not receive our witness. If I told you earthly things and you do not believe, how shall you believe if I tell you heavenly things? (John 3:10–12)

The main assumption in Israel was that the Messiah would be a political deliverer and leader. They were more concerned with the political and the temporal than the spiritual. Jesus's messiahship transcended the political landscape –– He came to set all people free from the bondage of sin and death, not just a small group from an oppressive government. This understanding was difficult for the Jews to accept and remains difficult even today. Jesus's conviction of the aspects of the kingdom of God were secure because He knew the Father, because He knew who He was, and because He saw the Kingdom of God in action through signs and wonders.

Another example is the story of when Moses sent out twelve spies into the land of Canaan, one from each of the tribes of Israel. Canaan was the land that God promised to give to the people of Israel (Num.13). After forty days, they returned to give their report. All twelve acknowledged that the land was wonderful and did indeed flow with "milk and honey" (v. 27). However, ten of the spies expressed doubt and fear that the inhabitants were too strong for Israel to conquer (vs. 27-29, 31-33), despite the fact that God promised them the land. Ten men influenced about 4.5 million people with their fear, doubt, rebellion, and negative comments. Just ten men! Group think occurred quickly due to corporate fear and rebellion.

No one listened to Joshua and Caleb who tried to assure the people that God was with them, and that the land would be theirs, despite the obstacles. God said of Caleb, that he had a "different spirit and has followed Me fully" (Num.14:24). That different spirit is what is needed to understand the truth. That different spirit breaks through fear, doubt, and rebellion. A different spirit does not live by assumptions, but by truth and faith in God and His Word. The ultimate result was that Joshua and Caleb were the only two people that were allowed to see the land, enter the land, and settle in the land with their descendants.

The alternative to assumptions is convictions. Convictions are developed personally and intrinsically and come through revelation and experience. A conviction is a convinced conscience. Being convinced requires transformation. Conviction is the transformation of conscience, not the convenience of assumptions. I found it very revealing that the word *conviction*, at least as we understand it, does not appear in the Hebrew Old Testament, outside of a reference in Job 32:12, which is more accurately rendered as "corrected." Other Old Testament words translated as "persuaded" are more accurately defined as "stirred up" or "enticed."

Satan's deception is often enticement — causing us to believe something is true because he has stirred up our emotions and has effectively deceived us. Over the last few years in our nation, our own communities have experienced this when certain events are used to stir us up and entice us into believing something is true when it is not. Much of the deception leads to the overlooking of what is really wrong – pride, rebellion, going against authority, entitlement thinking, and spiritual warfare. The enticement leads to further lawlessness, wrong thinking, and therefore wrong solutions.

However, in the New Testament, the root word for *convinced* in the Greek, *elegeho*, is used by Jesus. The apostle Paul especially, uses the word in much of his writings. It means, "to downright prove" or "to admonish; to correct; to convince." Another poignant understanding of this Greek word is, "to be quickened by life." Generally speaking, life tends to provide us with experiences that bring wisdom and therefore convictions that last. The life of Jesus also persuades us about God. Because of Jesus (God's "body language"), we can now be convinced of so many things about God, His love, His grace towards us, and His dealings with us. Paul writes in Romans 8:38–39:

> For I am convinced that neither death, nor life, nor angels, nor principalities, nor things present, nor things to come, nor powers, nor height, nor depth, nor any other created thing, shall be able to separate us from the love of God, which is in Christ Jesus our Lord.

There is a drastic difference between those who lived before Christ to absolutely understand in a convincing way the love of God and those who live after Christ, because God acted out His love through Jesus. The men and women in the Old Testament who lived a life of conviction dramatically stood out from among their contemporaries because they were so few in number. After Christ, we can more easily live with conviction because of what we know God did for us, and because of the explosion of the church through which the gospel spread, which continues today. The New Testament uses words like *persuaded* and *convinced* to indicate that a true change of thinking and behavior has occurred. We are more enticed today than we are convinced of anything. Conviction changes lives toward the truth –- enticement perpetuates lies and rebellion.

Conviction and convinced come from the same root word. Conviction is life changing. It is more than just believing something. James 2:19 says, "You believe that there is one God. You do well; the demons also believe, and shudder." Obviously, simply believing is not enough for a transformed life. Hebrews 11:1 declares, "Now faith is the *assurance* of things hoped for, the *conviction* of things not seen" (italics mine). Just because people attend church doesn't always mean a deep personal conviction or commitment. Assumptions just fill the void. Convictions transform the void. Wright states:

> It's simple. Conviction always moves us back to the Father. To say, "I am not worthy, so I will stay away from my Father," is shame. To say, "I am not worthy, but I will go to my Father," is conviction. . . Shame always causes us to feel more distant from God. Conviction always makes us feel closer to God (Wright, 2005, 84).

Agendas are not real convictions, as they tend to be self-centered concepts that would place someone in a good light among the masses. Convictions often go against the common wisdom of the contemporary culture, thus bringing anxiety and potential ridicule. Having an agenda will say, "Someone (or many someones) will approve of me, so I will choose to believe this or I will do this to be accepted." Having a conviction will say, "I know what is right in this matter, and while I know it will not bring me the most approval, I will do it anyway." In order to be convinced of anything, the truth of God has to exist. Once the truth emerges, understanding can be achieved, and the individuals involved are set right.

In the 2012 movie, *The Avengers*, produced by Marvel Studios, and distributed by Walt Disney Studios Motion Pictures, there is an exchange between Loki, Thor's evil brother who had an agenda and was the adversary of the super Heroes, and agent Phil Coleson, who works for the Government Intelligence Agency, an ally of the Avengers. Agent Phil is mortally wounded in a fight against Loki, and he has some final words for his enemy. Agent Phil is expressing confidence of their victory, even though the current state of the battle would show otherwise. The brief exchange went something like this:

Agent Phil –– "You are going to lose."

Loki –– "Am I? Your heroes are scattered. Your floating fortress falls from the sky. Where is my disadvantage?"

Agent Phil –– "You're gonna lose. It's in your nature. You lack conviction."

The truth is that living an authentic and realistic life is the deepest yearning of our soul and that no assumption will ever help us reach living a true, authentic life. The core longing of understanding is satisfied when we know the truth about who we are, about the ones with whom we have relationships, and about situations around us. Understanding God through faith and knowing that He understands us, also helps us develop an authentic lifestyle. Ruiz writes,

> Just imagine the day that you stop making assumption with your partner and eventually with everyone else in your life. Your way of communicating will change completely, and your relationships will no longer suffer from conflicts created by mistaken assumptions (Ruiz 1997, 71––72).

Perceptions

Perceptions are the eyes of assumptions. Once we assume something to be true, we then see things and people through the lenses of our assumptions, causing a perception. On the other hand, we may perceive something and render an assumption that is inaccurate because our perception was flawed. Perceptions can often be "a blanket statement," or a comprehensive assessment that leads to prejudice, hatred, or fear. These types of perceptions are often driven by relational hurt and bitterness. For example, perceptions that all Caucasians are racists; or that all police officers are corrupt; or that all pastors are after your money, or that all churches are the same, are just a few that are driven by past hurts and frustrations.

Mike and his wife, in their early thirties, came to counseling as a couple. They had been married for about five years and were having many conflicts, mostly over Mike's anger and perceptions of everyone rejecting him, no matter what he said or did. He had been in some counseling before but claimed no one ever was able to help him. As we delved into Mike's life over the first few weeks and the potential root of his deep-seeded anger, he forcefully declared, "No one in my family cared how I felt. And my mother died when I was seventeen, but you probably have no idea what that is like!"

Of all the ways I have been able to be empathetic with most people's issues and background, this one case was among the most congruent for me. In a rare expression of self-disclosure, I said, "Well, Mike, maybe I can understand, since I experienced the death of my mother also, when I was seventeen." I cannot describe how completely Mike's countenance changed at that moment. For a few moments he froze, then began to cry. He said, "Then there is someone who does know how I have felt for so many years." From that moment forward, Mike allowed me to pursue areas of his life and perceptions that no one else ever had. He had found someone (it was God's doing really) who he felt could truly understand him. That understanding was so important that his perception of himself and others began to take a dramatic turn.

Perceptions start within us and are formed through self-talk. Human beings have a tendency to be too introspective. Often introspection is critical, and we typically put ourselves down. Based upon certain assumptions about our own life and our past, we tend to be too heavy with negative self-talk. Introspection can be viewed as "coming alongside oneself." As a result, we are listening to just one voice and often times the wrong one. As we get used to negative self-talk, it usually turns into negative perceptions about others as well. We can only give that which we have.

Joey was in college and became depressed because he did not believe his parents understood him. He was an excellent soccer athlete with hopes of playing at the college level. However, he severely injured his knee as a high school senior during a game and was not able to play in college. Joey felt guilty because he felt he let his parents and his family down. He did not like being sad all the time, and he wanted his parents to know it wasn't their fault (this young man was totally projecting his own guilt onto his parents). He felt guilty that his parents continued to provide for his college, and he did not feel he deserved their help. Joey perceived that they felt the same way he did. I encouraged Joey *to ask* his parents about the issue. Once he learned that they sincerely did not feel as he did, his entire outlook and countenance changed, and he slowly began to see depression lift from his life and motivation return. Often perceptions are our own thoughts and feelings projected onto others, as if they were true.

It becomes critical to have the Holy Spirit, or as John calls Him, the Counselor or Helper (John 14:16), become the voice we hear. The Greek word for Counselor in this passage is *paracletos* which means, *one who comes along side of to help.* The Holy Spirit is the Spirit of truth (John 14:17), and it is essential to know the truth about what we assume, what we perceive, and who we are. The "paracletos" gives living counseling and living water from which to drink, which brings us into truth. The apostle John wrote:

> Beloved, if our heart does not condemn us, we have confidence
> before God; and whatever we ask, we receive from Him,
> because we keep His commandments and do the things that
> are pleasing in His sight. And this is His commandment, that
> we believe in the name of His Son Jesus Christ, and love one
> another, just as He commanded us. (1 John 3:21–23)

The young person might say, "My parents just don't know me" or "My parents don't understand who I am." Or any of us would simply declare, "You just don't understand!" On the other hand, the issue can be that the young person does not understand the intention behind why his or her parents say and do what they say and do. When we say that, or hear that, something is being ignored, miscommunicated, or not properly received. As a result, we form assumptions, and then we perceive to be true that which we assume. To break this pattern, we need to challenge our assumptions or be slow to assume. The result can be adjusted perceptions.

Intentions

Intentions form into behaviors. What we intend to do, we usually do. Assumptions and perceptions are formed in the mind. Intentions are formed in the heart. Assumptions and perceptions can be challenged and corrected. However, it takes great care to challenge and correct intentions, as they represent more of the core of the person.

In my experience, the most determining factor that leads to misunderstanding is the misreading of another person's intentions. When we believe we know what another person has in their heart, we can base our assumptions and perceptions on this factor. It is not wise to judge another person's actions until you know his or her motives or intentions. Essentially, we feel we know the other person's heart, which is a diabolical pattern that will surely distort our understanding. This is nothing new, as it actually began with how the serpent deceived Adam and Eve.

In Genesis 3:1--7, we read the story of the dialog between the serpent and the first couple. The crux of the message made by the serpent was:

- God is a liar ("You surely shall not die" -- v. 4).
- God is restrictive because He's threatened by you ("God knows that in the day you eat from it your eyes will be opened, and you will be like God" -- v. 5).
- God is withholding from you (When you eat from the tree, "You will be like God, knowing good and evil" and He obviously has kept that understanding from you -- v. 5).

All three lies were Satan's distorted renditions of God's true intentions toward His prized creation. Once Adam and Eve altered their understanding of God's intentions, they became self-oriented instead of God-oriented. They took for themselves and as a result, relationships, the world, their outlook on life, and feelings about God dramatically changed. All of which remain true for us today and in need of the redemptive power of Christ.

False beliefs about intentions will cause all kinds of conflict. The story about Lamont, in the beginning of this chapter, is one of countless examples I can provide. Often, conflicts in marriage are about one misreading or assuming the intent of the other. Conflicts between parents and their children are often about the misunderstanding of intentions. Children will assume their parents do not have their best interest in mind by virtue of rules, curfews, or restrictions. On the other hand, parents may miss the mark with their children's intentions when they don't trust their kids. It is essential to be sure of one's intentions.

When it seems like whatever we can do is better than those in authority over us, we begin to doubt their intentions. Wiser people and people of understanding often have a gained perspective that others may not have. Intentions could be that of protection, a need to wait until maturity or ability develops, or that of knowing what outcomes will occur. Love is God's intentions. Love is usually the intent behind good parents. To know another one's intention takes effort, attentiveness, and the application of truth. We may also need to simply ask, to provide the necessary understanding.

It is critical to believe the good intentions of those who love us. It is also critical to discern the unknown intentions of those who we may not know yet, or of those who have a reputation that is questionable. The Word of God can be our guide, as Hebrews 4:12 states, "For the Word of God is living and active" –- (remember Jesus is the Word in the flesh, God's body language, and He is living and active today!) –- "And sharper than any two-edged sword . . . able to judge the thoughts and intentions of the heart."

Often, misunderstandings place us in a defensive situation, trying to defend the *intent* of our heart and *intent* of our behavior. Once again, if there is a misreading of someone's *intent*, you can be sure the devil is behind such doubt and is whispering lies. I counsel couples to be very careful not to misread their spouse's *intent*. In conflict, once intentions are questioned, the actual issue of conflict becomes secondary and personal names are brandished back and forth. Such conflict is not a good way to reach resolution. Do not be so quick to assume someone's intent. All behaviors have intentions that drive them. Behaviors with bad intentions will more often than not cause harm. However, behaviors with good intentions do not always succeed. Experiencing a bad outcome does not mean there were bad intentions. We need to be careful not to assume that negative intentions are present behind every behavior.

CHAPTER 6
Hindrances to Understanding

How much better it is to get wisdom than gold! And
to get understanding is to be chosen above silver.

— Prov. 16:16

And he gave me instruction and talked with me, and
said, "O Daniel, I have now come forth to give you insight
with understanding.

— Daniel 9:22

Trust in the Lord with all your heart, and do not lean
on your own understanding.

— Prov. 3:5

From 1982 until 1993, the Columbia Broadcasting System (CBS),
aired a situational comedy called *Cheers*. The fictitious setting
was that of a tavern in Boston, Massachusetts. It was a very popular
weekly show. The theme song of the show, "Where Everybody Knows
Your Name" became a feel-good song of the show. Written by Judy
Hart-Angelo and Gary Portnoy, the song generates a perfect segue

into the setting of the show --- a bar where many come to tell their troubles, and receive understanding and acceptance. The chorus of the song is especially pertinent to our discussion here:

> Sometimes you want to go,
> Where everybody knows your name,
> And they're always glad you came;
> You want to be where you can see,
> Our troubles are all the same;
> You want to be where everybody knows your name.

To feel like everyone knows you, listens to you, sees you as you are, shares your struggles, and accepts you are just some of the aspects that describe the core longing to be understood. "We impress people with our strength, but we connect with our weakness" (Weece 2016, 10). It has often been said that bars or taverns are such places to find understanding. Often, places like these can provide a sense of belonging as well. It should be the church and the people of God. As a result, I believe we as Christians have some work to do.

Jacob, a young college student had difficulty in the past with drinking and marijuana, but had remained completely sober for more than two years. He also was shy, with a good heart for others, and a brilliant student, studying for two majors. He also had the experiences of being bullied when in elementary school and early middle school, mostly as a result of being skinny and so smart. Over time, Jacob learned that he was not understood. Others were not able to keep up in conversations with him, so he was often left to himself. He desired so much to have friends who understood him. Jacob began a relationship with a girl early in college who trusted him with traumatic experiences in her life that she had not told anyone. They eventually began dating. That made Jacob feel good, as if what was being said was, "She understands me and knows I am trustworthy and care about her feelings and about her secrets. I am not just an egghead. She sees that I care about people too."

When she turned on him and accused him of something he did not do, he felt hurt, then angry and the sense of being understood quickly went up in smoke. Soon after their argument, Jacob went to a party and got drunk, after being away from that scene for more than two years. Once his girlfriend found out about his drunken episode, she said, "See, I knew you wanted to hurt me, and now you're doing it again by drinking again." Jacob's deficiency in feeling understood, because of the false accusation, drove him to either obtain understanding on his own power, (by hanging with people who were drinking and also who he believed understood him), or at least medicate the pain of not being understood. Feeling hurt and bitter can cloud our understanding of self and others. Being understood is to know that we are seen. Being seen for who we are is a wonderful, fulfilling feeling.

As Jacob and I processed through his reaction to his girlfriend, and how his core longing of being understood was not met, he was encouraged to express to her how he felt in their relationship. He regained a positive perspective on who he was as a person and an affirmation as to his intentions, which helped Jacob regain new motivation to avoid the drinking and pursue his real passion in life. Even though Jacob and his girlfriend came to a better understanding of one another, and talked things out, they eventually agreed to end their dating relationship.

Today, a lack of understanding, decreased critical thinking skills, lingering bitterness, arriving at judgments much too fast, emotional-only perspectives, and ignoring rational thinking have become prominent. As a result, many people tune out and avoid wisdom and instead are choosing to lean on their own understanding. The great hindrances to understanding are lack of foresight, assumptions that masquerade as convictions, personal agendas, over-dependence upon emotions, a need for training and being enlightened, trials and difficult circumstances, over-emphasis on pleasure-seeking, bitterness, self-centeredness, rebellion, and wounds of the soul.

In Paul's letter to Timothy, he provides a list of things that impact our ability to understand:

> But realize this, that in the last days difficult times will come. For men will be lovers of self, lovers of money, boastful, arrogant, revilers, disobedient to parents, ungrateful, unholy, unloving, irreconcilable, malicious gossips, without self-control, brutal, haters of good, treacherous, reckless, conceited, lovers of pleasure rather than lovers of God; holding to a form of godliness, although they have denied its power . . . *always learning and never able to come to the knowledge of the truth.* (2 Tim. 3:1–7, *italics* mine)

If we meditate on any of these concepts, it becomes quite clear that they all have a way of clouding our ability to understand God, each other, and the world around us. Understanding requires humility, "and humility isn't thinking less of yourself. Humility is thinking of yourself less" (Weece 2016, 51). As mentioned earlier, true understanding leads us to God, and from God greater understanding is attained. None of the attitudes and behaviors listed in the above biblical passage can do that. Even some forms of godliness, albeit our own way of defining it, deny the Holy Spirit's power to transform.

I believe we are in a time of great confusion, rebellion, lawlessness, cynicism, emotional woundedness, disillusionment, and spiritual warfare. More and more people are disappointed, feeling hurt, and angry. Knee-jerk and emotional reactions are patterns in our day that do not allow for the time needed to truly understand a person or a situation. As a result, understanding one another, the time in which we live, and the ways of God, have become clouded and difficult. Understanding requires us to slow down, think, and truly consider. Cultural differences are ignored. Experiential differences are not considered. Gender differences are denied and being altered with the misinterpreting of science as a springboard into androgynous concepts.

The prevailing desire to try to make everyone the same has undermined our God-given differences, resulting in frustrating misunderstandings. To assume that every one is the same is much too simplistic, and is not required to obtain understanding. We are different in temperaments, personalities, experiences, genetics, and cultural influences, just to name a few. It is essential to acknowledge existing differences and to not simply ignore distinctions.

However, there are similarities that all human being have. We are sinners and have fallen short of the glory of God (Rom. 3:23). We have all been disappointed and hurt in life somewhere and somehow. We have all come from a not-so-perfect home. It is because we all live in a fallen and broken world. G. K. Chesterton said, "Christianity with a surer and more reverent realism says that we are all fools. This doctrine is sometimes called the doctrine of original sin. It may also be described as the doctrine of the equality of man" (Belmonte 2011, 196).

We are all comprised of brokenness and beauty. The good news is that Jesus makes no distinction as to whom He loves and pursues. Romans 10:12--13 states, "For there is no distinction between Jew and Greek; for the same Lord is Lord of *all*, abounding in riches for *all* who call upon Him; for *whoever* will call upon the Name of the Lord will be saved" (*italics* mine). Every one of us also needs Jesus as our Savior, Healer, and Lord.

We need to celebrate diversity, but not to the extent of drawing lines in the sand to separate people. Understanding one another, in its true spirit, is to draw together. Age differences can be honored. I was always taught as a youngster to respect my elders and those in authority. Older people should appreciate youthful exuberance and perspective, as long as they do not include rebellion and disrespect. The nuances of racial and ethnic differences can be respected, but it requires time in relationship, dialog, and understanding with no assumptions and agendas. Gender differences between men and women can enhance relationships in dating and marriages, once they are understood.

For example, there are distinct differences between the male and female brain. Dr. Carolyn Leaf has studied the human brain for most of her career. She describes some basic differences between men and women that are physiological and genetic. For example:

- The male brain is 9 percent larger than the female brain, but with the same nerve cells. Female brains are more densely packed due to a slightly smaller skull.
- The insula -- the center that processes gut feelings -- is larger and more active in women than men.
- The hippocampus -- which deals with short-term memory and memory processing -- is estrogen sensitive and is larger and more active in women than in men.
- The corpus callosum -- area of brain responsible for thinking processes -- is C-shaped in men and hour-glass shaped in women. Men have more focused thinking, and women have

more multi-task thinking. (However, too much multi-task leads to frazzledness.)

- Women can read body language better than men. Women pick up sadness 90 percent of the time; men pick up sadness 40 percent of the time.
- Men build self-esteem through maintaining independence; and women through dependence.
- When at rest, 70 percent of men's electrical brain activity is shut down; 30 percent of female's electrical brain activity is shut down.
- Women tend to have a wider peripheral vision, and men can see more clearly and accurately ahead over longer distances.
- Women can typically hear better than men, but men are better at locating where the sound is coming from.
- Men need more touch –– women have more of the bonding hormone, oxytocin, and are ten times more sensitive to touch. As a result, men typically need to be touched two to three times more often than women.
- Men are "internal processors" and women are "external processors." Helps explain why women need to verbally process in order to come to a decision and men prefer to contemplate.
- The area of the brain for communication and words is 11 percent larger in females than in males (Leaf, 2009).

These are just some of the many differences between men and women that affect the ability to understand one another. Differences are created by God in order for the uniting of a husband and wife, two genders becoming one, to be a complete representation of God. God's nature is found uniquely and distinctively in both men and women, and both genders are equally created in God's image. The two genders are to be celebrated and understood, not altered into androgynous concepts. The brokenness of sin has altered the ability of being one in marriage, and having the understanding needed in relationships. It is critical, therefore, to have Jesus involved in the joining of a man and a woman in marriage.

Bridgett enjoyed sexual intimacy with her husband. She desired sex at least a couple of times per week. Her husband was less interested. Bridgett's background was the oldest of four children, with three younger brothers. Her parents required her to take care of her brothers, and when her mother died before her adolescent years, her dad increased that expectation. She grew up believing that she had to take care of everyone else, and be there for whoever needed her. The intimacy Bridgett longed for with her husband, while enjoyable, actually represented something much more beyond the physical sex act. Having sex with her husband was a time for her. It was a time that made her feel special and cared for –- a time where someone was attentive and expressing love to her in an intimate and meaningful way. When we discussed this aspect, Bridgett wept and said it was a revelation to understand herself more, and wonderful to know someone else understood her. We discussed this with her husband as well, and he grew to appreciate her need and learned to help his wife feel special. He also learned and became attentive to other ways to help her feel valued. The understanding provided healing to her and their relationship.

In his book *The Five Love Languages*, Gary Chapman wrote about ways that people communicate love. There is often a disconnect that occurs when we attempt to receive love the same way we express it. The five love languages are: words of affirmation; physical touch; acts of service; giving and receiving gifts; and quality time (Chapman

2015). We naturally flow in our love language, but often struggle showing love using another's love language. What my primary love language is may not be yours, and as a result we may experience a misunderstanding of showing love and the receiving of love.

In my own counselor training, I had to grow in areas to which I was not exposed in order to develop understanding and be effective. I learned every culture has a "language," and it is important to understand the language. Multi-cultural training and experience was one area in which I gained competence. Non-ethnic cultures like those who serve as police officers, firefighters, nurses, clergy, and mental health professionals, for example, also have a language based on their distinct training and unique experience. Another area is the military.

I always have had a tremendous respect for the men and women who serve in our military as they are the keepers and the defenders of our nation and the freedoms we all enjoy. So, when I had the opportunity to serve those who serve us as a Christian counselor, I enthusiastically jumped at the chance, and became a TRICARE and Military One Source (MOS) provider. I spent several years counseling military personnel and their families near Fort Bragg, North Carolina, at an off-post Christian Counseling agency. My clinical director was a licensed counselor but also a retired lieutenant colonel, serving twenty-nine years as an Army Ranger. He became a mentor and a friend. I learned a great deal under his leadership.

As I embarked upon the ministry of counseling military servicemen and servicewomen, I found that I was not as prepared as I thought I was. I came across individuals who were trained in Special Operations, Special Forces, and Army Airborne. From Fort Bragg, many were coming and going from multiple deployments. Their families had to deal with the various stressors of conducting life without their spouses, parents, or children, as well as the constant concerns for their loved ones' safety. What I did not understand was how unique the challenges were to military personnel and their families. For me, my father had been about ten years removed from military life as a World War II combat Marine by the time I was born.

The military life, one of countless acronyms, abbreviations, unique lingo, different lifestyle, and a special mind-set, was one that I did not know nor had I ever experienced. At first, my assumptions and counseling approach and training left a lot to be desired. I enjoyed success as a Christian counselor and minister with other populations prior to coming to the Fort Bragg community, so I assumed I would see similar outcomes. It took me several months, before I realized that I was not connecting with my military clients like I needed to and my lack of effectiveness was becoming a personal discouragement. I simply did not understand the soldier.

I began to seek the advice of my clinical director (and I prayed a lot!). We started to spend a great deal of time together as he educated me about today's military life style and nuances. He shared his experiences as an Army Ranger and as a counselor. I began to see certain things that would help me connect with my clients, even though I never served in the military myself. After a few months of his (and God's) impartation, if you will, I began to experience a drastic change in my effectiveness. I learned to understand the military experience as best I could, and to ask questions of my military clients, who were glad to enlighten me. The more I asked, the more I learned. The more I learned, the more empathetic I became, as I needed to remain humble, unassuming, and respectful to the military service member.

My understanding of the specific culture of military life increased, and as a result, I became a viable, trusted, and effective counselor for the military population. Eventually, the ultimate compliment came one day when my clinical director introduced me to a pastor friend of his, who was a career military officer, by saying of me, "He is just like us, he just didn't serve." While I understood the compliment as I learned to speak the language, I do not at all pretend to understand everything about military life and combat experience. I am very aware that I have not experienced what military service is like and will fall short at times.

Emotions

Emotions can tend to throw us off. They can impede understanding if we feel more strongly than what reality presents. On the other hand, we tend to also discard emotions completely, often believing that they are not to be considered. We need to understand that all humans are physical, intellectual, spiritual, and emotional beings. To ignore, diminish, or discard any of these components, reduces us to something less than the total person we are. For example, one mistake couples often make is to say to one another, "You can't feel that way" or "Stop feeling that way" or "How can you possibly feel that way?" The best way to address emotions is to validate them.

To validate people's emotions is to acknowledge how they feel and their perspective. It can lead to an opportunity to understand them. Validating sounds something like, "I see that you felt upset about what I did." Or, "I understand how you would feel that way. Please let me explain." Or, "That must have been horrible for you to experience." Validating is recognizing that someone has emotions and how they may have been affected. Validating is not necessarily agreement. Nor is it caving in or ignoring our own emotions. It is keeping the defensive walls from forming and opening up communication to allow for understanding to take place.

Likewise, it is also critical to validate and recognize our own emotions. To ignore and repress emotions only brings harm to us. We need to be in safe relationships that allow, even invite, the ability of each person to express how we feel. "Many people want intimacy. Few people understand that intimacy requires vulnerability" (Weece 2016, xvi). For example, it is healthy to say, "When I heard you say that I messed up, I felt rejected." The focus is on what you heard and your feelings, which can be more disarming than accusing someone of hurting you. Defensive walls go up when we feel accused. Defensive walls can remain down when we can suggest how we felt. The ability to understand and recover is increased when both parties have the freedom to be heard and be clarified.

Children who understood that they were to be "seen and not heard" may be among the children who felt they could not speak up and tell someone that they were being sexually or physically abused. That is part of the tragedy of abuse. Abuse is devastating to the victim. Add to the actual abuse the belief that they have no voice and no one will listen, and a sense of feeling alone, powerless, and hopelessness can occur.

The Bible gives a dramatic example of repressed feelings. Second Samuel 13 describes the events leading up to and after King David's daughter, Tamar, was raped by her half-brother Amnon. When Tamar's full brother, Absalom, learned of the abuse he said to Tamar, "'Has Amnon your brother been with you? But now keep silent, my sister, he is your brother; do not take this matter to heart.' So Tamar remained and was desolate in her brother Absalom's house" (2 Sam 13:20). The word desolate here in Hebrew meant that Tamar remained broken, ruined, and empty. She was never given the opportunity to feel understood. It is part of the healing process to put language to an event!

One way that depression has been defined is, *anger turned inward*. Psalm 31:10 says, "For my life is spent with grief, and my years with sighing: my strength faileth because of mine iniquity, and my bones are consumed" (KJV). Also, Proverbs 17:22 declares, "A joyful heart is good medicine, but a broken spirit dries up the bones." Emotional and mental wounds have been shown to affect us physiologically. Conditions like ulcers, high blood pressure, and diabetes, just to name a few, have been linked to depression and bipolar disorders. Validating our own feelings is not only emotionally and mentally healthy, but can be physically healthy as well.

Sometimes we are afraid of emotions. Perhaps that was the case with Job's friends. In the biblical story of Job, he had three friends who attempted to help him. Eliphaz, Bildad, and Zophar came together, "to come to sympathize with him and comfort him" (Job 2:11). They, "sat down on the ground with him for seven days and seven nights with no one speaking a word to him, for they saw that his pain was very great" (Job 2:13). To remain silent was the best thing they did for Job. After that time, each one made feeble attempts and long discourses to try to explain how and why Job's suffering came to be, as most of the book of Job records. None of what they said was helpful or accurate about Job, his suffering, and especially God, in the midst of suffering. Job 42:7 records God's response:

> And it came about after the Lord had spoken these words to Job, that the Lord said to Eliphaz the Temanite, "my wrath is kindled against you and against your two friends, because you have not spoken of me what is right as My servant Job has."

In our attempts to understand loss and suffering, our tendency is to want to know and explain the hows and the whys. When people have experienced loss and suffering, the best thing we can do is give them our presence -- many times with no words, except that of encouragement. When I have come along side wounded people, it is amazing to me how they are so thankful when I have not necessarily done very much. They felt understood simply by my presence and my concern.

I remember a few days after my father died, a man came over to me after a church meeting and simply sat with me and cried with me -- no words were spoken. I can't tell you how much that meant at the time. I felt totally understood. To try and provide some understanding in the middle of the tragic event or crisis would only have exacerbated the pain and frustration. Romans 12:15 suggests perhaps the best advice to create an atmosphere of understanding: "Rejoice with those who rejoice, and weep with those who weep."

Strong emotions affect our memories as well. The relationship between emotion and memory is complex, but generally, emotion tends to increase the likelihood that *an event* will be remembered later and that it will be remembered vividly. Episodic or "flashbulb" memory is one example of this. Some examples of this would be an experience such as a close family member dying, when the space shuttle *Challenger* exploded, when the terrorists attack on 9/11 took place, or the Christmas that you got the exact toy you wanted as a kid. The experience holds so much emotional significance that it is encoded as an extremely vivid, almost picture-perfect memory.

Emotions, such as shame, fear, guilt, euphoria, celebration, and loss, just to name a few, may lead to vivid recall of the event due to having the experience etched in our memory. These "episodic memories" are memories of personal events (times, places, associated emotions, and other contextual who, what, when, where, why knowledge) that can be explicitly stated. It is the collection of past personal experiences that occurred at a particular time and place. For example, if you remember the party on your sixth birthday, this is an episodic memory. They allow you to figuratively travel back in time to remember the event that took place at that particular time and place (Schacter, 2011).

Events that are recorded into episodic memory may trigger episodic learning such as a change in behavior that occurs as a result of an event (Terry, 2006). These learned behaviors and developing belief systems are not always an accurate representation of what it is that we needed to learn. While the event maybe recalled accurately, the *interpretation of the event* is distorted if we rely only on emotions to interpret. Often, emotions can develop into perceptions that are not accurate. Emotions can often distort, and even fabricate a memory. For example, a fear of dogs after being bitten by a dog is a result of episodic learning. A person may surmise that all dogs are mean and dangerous and that they need to keep their distance. Of course, not all dogs are mean and dangerous, but changing a person's understanding can be difficult. Other examples of resulting assumptions based on episodic memories are as follows:

- All men are abusers
- All women are gossips
- All whites are racists
- All minorities are thugs
- All pastors are power-hungry
- All churches are the same
- All teenagers get into trouble

These are just some of many other blanket statements and beliefs. These generalizations are assumptions formed based upon experiences, which are not accurate, but unfortunately develop into personal belief systems, as we discussed earlier.

Retrieval is a process of reconstructing past experiences; this phenomenon of reconstruction is influenced by a number of different variables. Contextual effects occur as a result of the degree of similarity between the encoding context and the retrieval context of an emotional dimension. The main findings are that the current mood we are in affects what is attended, encoded, and ultimately retrieved, as reflected in two similar but subtly different effects: the mood congruence effect and mood-state dependent retrieval.

The mood congruence effect refers to the tendency of individuals to retrieve information more easily when it has the same emotional content as their current emotional state. For instance, being in a depressed mood increases the tendency to remember negative events (Watkins, et al., 1996). Memory recall tends to be congruent with one's current mood, with depressed people more likely to recall negative events from the past (Hertel, 2004). In addition, depression is often associated with poor memory. It appears that memories of past emotional responses are not always accurate, and can even be partially reconstructed based on their current appraisal of events (Levine and Pizarro, 2004).

Pride and arrogance are hindrances to understanding. When we believe we have what it takes to get the job done, when in reality we do not, we often find failure instead. Proverbs 14:12, says, "There is a way which seems right to a man, but its end is the way of death."

Bitterness is an emotional state that appears to energize an individual, but in reality it actually drains the person. The deception is that by holding onto bitterness we are rendering power over the other person. The reality is that bitterness actually develops power over us. Hebrews 12:15 implores us, "See to it . . . that no root of bitterness springing up causes trouble, and by it many be defiled." There is no peace or justice in bitterness. The dictionary defines bitterness as, "causing or showing sorrow or pain." Bitterness actually can become one's identity. Wardle says, "When they try to exact payback and protection by withholding forgiveness, wounded people only add more destructive darkness to their already broken lives." (Wardle 2001, 206). The apostle Paul in Romans 12:17--21 clearly states:

> Never pay back evil for evil to anyone. Respect what is right in the sight of all men. If possible, so far as it depends on you, be at peace with all men. Never take your own revenge, but leave room for the wrath of God, for it is written, "Vengeance is Mine, I will repay," says the Lord. "But if your enemy is hungry, feed him, and if he is thirsty, give him a drink; for in so doing you will heap burning coals upon his head." Do not be overcome by evil, but overcome evil with good.

The law of reciprocity has been established by God. In other words, one will reap what one sows. Galatians 6:7--9 states:

> Do not be deceived, God is not mocked; for whatever a man sows, this he will also reap. For the one who sows to his own flesh shall from the flesh reap corruption, but the one who sows to the Spirit shall from the Spirit reap eternal life. And let us not lose heart in doing good, for in due time we shall reap if we do not grow weary.

To be at peace with all men requires that we release our bitterness, forgive, and give up our rights to revenge. No revenge is necessary on our part. Instead, if we allow good to overcome evil, then we are truly defined by strength, not weakness. Even if we do take revenge, how can we tell when enough revenge is sufficient? What is used to measure whether an offense has been satisfied? More often than not, there is never enough payback to satisfy the offense, especially as long as we hold onto bitterness. As a result, peace and freedom are not achieved through revenge. It is like drinking poison and expecting the other person to die. Unless we walk in forgiveness, it is difficult to understand others, ourselves, and situations.

Luke 24:13–35 provides a good example of how emotions blind our ability to understand and see clearly. The emotions portrayed in this story can be identified as primarily grief, depression, and anger, leading to cynicism, lack of understanding, and ignoring what our spirits may be telling us. The men in this story are blinded by the dark -- the darkness of their sorrow. It isn't until these men experienced Jesus through the bread and the wine, that they saw Him clearly.

The scene is just after the crucifixion of Jesus, and Jesus has already been raised from the dead. There are two men, followers of Jesus, on the road to Emmaus, a small village outside of Jerusalem. They are walking the day of Jesus's resurrection, leaving town hearing that others had found the tomb empty, but apparently not believing that He had risen. As they were walking and discussing all the events that had just taken place, Jesus appeared and approached them and began walking with them. Their eyes were "prevented" from recognizing Him (v. 16), and Jesus began to converse with them. Jesus asked them what they were talking about, and "they stood still, looking sad" (v. 17). It is clear these men were grieving and depressed, and actually stopped in their tracks so abruptly, perhaps with some indignation, because they could not believe that the man who joined them seemingly had no idea what had happened in Jerusalem.

The answer they gave Jesus had the spirit of cynicism. Verse 18 records the answer one of the men gave to Jesus, "Are you the only one visiting Jerusalem and unaware of the things which have happened here in these days?" The men were flabbergasted that someone had no idea what had happened. Jesus asked in verse 19, "What things?" The men continued to describe what took place leading up to the crucifixion and that women and other disciples witnessed the empty tomb and that the angels said Jesus was alive (vs. 19–-24). These men, like others, assumed that Jesus "was going to redeem Israel" (v. 21), and they were sorrowful that He seemingly was not the Messiah after all. Their wrong assumptions, along with their grief and indignation, prevented them from understanding that it was the risen Jesus who was speaking to them! This is true today as well.

Jesus then declared in verse 25–-26, "O foolish men and slow of heart to believe in all that the prophets had spoken!" He began to tell these men what Moses and all the prophets had said about Him (v. 27). As they approached the village, they arrived at their destination. Jesus made it appear that He was going to continue, but they asked Him to stay with them. Apparently, their entire countenance, not to mention their opinion of the stranger, had changed. They walked with Him and talked with Him, and His presence and words transformed their demeanor from indignance to acceptance. The men even wanted Jesus to stay with them. It wasn't until Jesus broke bread and blessed it, and shared it with the men, (vs. 30-31), that they recognized who he was! In verse thirty-two, the men declared, "And they said to one another, 'Were not our hearts burning within us while He was speaking to us on the road, while He was explaining the Scriptures to us?' " It was their encounter with Jesus that transformed what was blocking their understanding and allowed them to see Jesus, resurrected and real.

This in just one of several occasions that show how our preoccupation in our emotions, in our work, or in ourselves in general can blind us from understanding what is the truth around us. The two men on their walk to Emmaus, and Mary Magdalene in the garden, were so preoccupied with their sorrow, they could not recognize Jesus standing next to them. Peter, James, and John had trouble enduring with Jesus in prayer in the Garden of Gethsemane as they kept falling asleep because of their deep sorrow (Luke 22:45). The fishermen-disciples on the lake were so preoccupied with their work that the presence of Jesus was obscured. The risen Christ will surely fulfil his own words, "The pure in heart, they shall see God" but only the pure in heart (Pulpit Commentary, 2010).

It is imperative that we address our anger, cynicism, bitterness, emotional hurt, and assumptions so that a pure heart can be restored and we can see clearly that which is true. Clarity of mind and emotions will bring clarity of spirit and bring understanding and wisdom to our lives. We spend too much time, polishing our shackles, instead of breaking them. Holding on to the past, keeps us in bondage and grieving, hindering our ability to see clearly. We hold onto ended chapters, but we need to move into the next chapter every time.

I encourage you to seek whatever prevents the purity and clarity of heart. Recognize your blind spots, based upon emotions, deception, assumptions, prejudices, and biases. Ask for help to remove them if need be, and be receptive to hear from others what needs to change. Do not feel judged if changes are legitimately needed and someone you trust speaks into your life. Freedom and clarity are the reward. You deserve to see clearly that which relates to God, others, and yourself!

CHAPTER 7
Misunderstood Labels and Names

A scoffer seeks wisdom, and finds none, but knowledge is easy to him who has understanding.

– Proverbs 14:6

For the Lord gives wisdom; from His mouth come understanding and wisdom.

– Proverbs 2:6 (NIV)

Who because of practice have their senses trained to discern good and evil.

– Hebrews 5:14

We have followed politicians, sports stars, and movie stars over the years. In our culture, we tend to watch and listen to what they do and say, both good and bad. We have heard so many prominent people make claims that they "misspoke" or what was said, "was taken out of context" or "misunderstood." On these occasions, the individual is trying to cover his or her mistakes. It can be an attempt to deflect sincere apology or repentance. They may have meant what they said at the time, but now are looking for ways to sidestep their comments. They would often blame the "receiver" for the miscommunication rather than themselves. The purpose may be to prevent being defined by their statements or behaviors.

There are times, however, that legitimate miscommunication does take place. Understanding and intent, as we have discussed earlier, are common aspects that lead to disconnects when people are communicating.

For example, let us consider a statement made by Jesus, found in Luke 7:31--35:

> To what then shall I compare the men of this generation, and what are they like? They are like children who sit in the market place and call to one another, and they say, "We played the flute for you, and you did not dance; we sang a dirge, and you did not weep." For John the Baptist has come eating no bread and drinking no wine, and you say, "He has a demon!" The Son of Man has come eating and drinking, and you say, "Behold a gluttonous man and a drunkard, a friend of tax collectors and sinners!" Yet wisdom is vindicated by all her children.

The religious people of Jesus's day were steeped in legalism and traditions of men. As a result, they found themselves bound and unable in their attempt to *define* Jesus and His works. The above account is an excellent example.

John the Baptist was ridiculed because he did not eat and drink like the religious folks of the day. It was claimed that he had a demon. Jesus, on the other hand, would eat and drink like the religious folks, but He ate and drank with people who were deemed as less desirable. As a result, He was called a glutton and drunkard.

The connotation was, had Jesus eaten and drank with the religious people, He would have been just fine. However, the religious people used one measuring stick, if you will, but developed two contrasting and conflicting views -- a double standard. Having it both ways gets people in trouble. When we compare others to standards that are set up by men, the result is misunderstanding and misjudged intentions. Jesus was mocked; His fellowship with sinners was mocked; His doctrine was (and is) mocked; His supernatural powers were (and are) mocked. He did not live according to the understanding and expectations of others. Those who follow after Jesus will experience similar things. Inaccurate names and identities soon follow.

In Luke 15:35, Jesus was saying that wisdom and truth always emerge, even though it may take a long time. Wisdom has offspring. There are positive outcomes to the expression and adherence to wisdom. One way to say the same thing in the vernacular is "The proof is in the pudding." The truth may take years to become evident. In the meantime, the best posture to take is to know the truth about who you are and your intentions, to live consistently to who you are, choose what you want not what you don't want, communicate clearly your desires and intentions, and most importantly, remain connected to your heavenly Father, in whose Name you ultimately exist. It is not just death and taxes that are inevitable. I believe the *truth always* has a way of rising to the top and showing forth its eventual results.

I would like to provide several very common characteristics that are often misunderstood and mislabeled when seen on the surface. Such characteristics can lead people to incorrectly identify someone. The truths about certain personalities, temperaments, intentions of the heart, and standing with God should always be considered as an antidote for misunderstandings.

The first description is of a *strong leader* with convictions. It is often true that many strong leaders have a problem with pride. God promises to deal with them if that is true (Prov. 16:18). However, there is a difference between pride and ego. Pride believes that we are more than we really are; that we are stronger than we really are; that we are more important than others; and that we build ourselves up as we put others down. The Bible is very clear that we should lay down our pride and arrogance before it destroys us. There is no place for arrogance in the Kingdom of God.

Ego, on the other hand, is simply a sense of self. A *healthy* sense of self is essential to our identity, (see *Created for Significance*), especially if we rest our identity in God. However, having a distorted ego can either lead to pride or to a low self worth. Paul states in Romans 12:3:

> For through the grace given to me I say to everyone among you *not to think more highly of himself than he ought to think*; but to think so as to have *sound judgment*, as God has allotted to each a measure of faith. (*italics* mine)

To have a sound, positive sense of self is healthy as long as we do not become narcissistic. Sound judgment about one's self is to know who you are, to know how much you need Jesus, your Savior every day, to know that ultimately you belong to God and He redeemed you, and feeling comfortable and confident in your own skin. Thinking of ourselves more highly than we ought leads to pride, which clouds our ability to understand others.

A strong leader with convictions does not have to be seen as someone with pride. Nor should he or she be seen as someone who is controlling. He or she may simply have a healthy ego, knowing one's identity and what the right thing to do would be. Such a person is often misunderstood. A good leader has a solid self-worth, self-awareness, and wisdom, yet enough humility to know when to admit wrong. For Christians, as long as we remain dependent upon Christ, our convictions of who He is can be reflected in us. The misjudgment occurs when a strong leader is called prideful when in reality he or she is walking in confidence.

Confidence is not to be confused with conceitedness. As we have seen earlier, the Greek word for "conceit" is *tuphoo* which means, "to wrap up in smoke." Arrogant or prideful people are clouded. They cannot see clearly because they are "wrapped up in smoke". They cannot see beyond themselves. G.K. Chesterton once said, "Surely the vilest point of human vanity is exactly that; to ask to be admired for admiring what your admirers do not admire" (Belmonte 2011, 217). Arrogant people are so wrapped up in themselves, that they can no longer hear God and usually tune out others. Such an individual is confined to their own conceit and does not see accurately. A false cloud equals false glory! Our glory and strength come from the Lord. Do not fall into the trap of shrinking back because others will classify you as prideful. Let the name of the Lord be your identity, and walk in the identity He gave you. Understand that ultimately your strength and abilities come from the Lord. If you are sincere in your submission to God, then confidence in Him can eliminate conceitedness in self.

The next description is of people who *take care of themselves.* Many may see such a person as self-absorbed or self-centered. Such a person is also viewed as not caring about others. While this may be true of some people, it is not always true. The Bible clearly warns us about being self-absorbed. Philippians 2:3--4 says, "Do nothing from selfishness or empty conceit, but with humility of mind regard one another as more important than yourselves; do not merely look out for your own interests, but also for the interest of others." To be a blessing to others is our calling, but we need to remember that we can only give that which we have.

Many caregivers, such as nurses, doctors, ministers, business owners, psychiatrists, and counselors, are notorious for draining themselves as they serve others. Some of these professionals are heavy smokers, overweight, and generally in bad health. In fact, physicians have the highest suicide rate among the helping professions (Foster and Shrira, 2009). Many professionals care for others more readily than they care for themselves, which is viewed as an honorable concept. Currently, it is being considered throughout the professional licensing boards of the fifty states to require a class on self-care as a requirement toward license renewal.

Sometimes the church and religious organizations can be among the most demanding of our time, efforts, and devotion. Self-care is often misunderstood as laziness and unwillingness. It is absolutely true that we should desire to serve God with the gifts and talents He has given. Such service is a manifestation of our redemption. However, such service does not enhance our redemption. Our redemption is a gift through Jesus. Our service to Him should come from gratitude and love. It is commonly assumed that the more we do, the more Christian we are. That understanding is not true.

We need to understand that no one is called to do it all. We are to operate within our gifts, be faithful to use our gifts for the common good, but be free to say "No" without criticism and guilt. Setting healthy boundaries does not mean we are lousy servants of God, or that we are disrespectful to the leaders. We are told when we serve to do so with excellence. In order to serve with excellence, self-care is required, so that we can be at our best when we are called upon.

In addition, no one should be expected to serve out of compulsion, guilt, or manipulation. Colossians 3:23 says, "Whatever you do, do your work heartily, as for the Lord rather than for men." "Whatever" does not mean "all." It refers to when we do choose to work, we should do so by giving our best in what we do. Churches, Christian schools and organizations need to adjust the way they "demand" service from their people simply because they can assume Christians want to serve God. That borders on exploitation.

However, if we look at the effectiveness of successful people, it is usually found that they know who they are, know their limits, are able to stay within their limitations, and work hard. This is an important part of self-care. As I take continuing education credits to keep my counseling license active, I have found a growing number of classes being offered dealing with self-care of the professional. The term *compassion fatigue* is a current description for burnout. We need to understand that self-care is not necessarily selfishness. Self-care is critical for the continued excellence in which anyone serves.

The Bible is not without examples of self-care either. In 2 Samuel 30:6, David is described as strengthening himself. During Jesus's earthly ministry, He often went off away from the crowds, and even from His disciples, in order to pray to the Father. He knew He needed to remain connected to the Father, the true source of His love and power, in order to continue ministering to the people and to follow through with His mission. He also needed time away from the growing, constant demands of the people. The more Jesus became known, the more attention He received. The more He gave and ministered, the more others wanted from Him. He understands the demands people place upon those who especially serve others. He truly understands, and I believe would endorse, if we were take time to replenish ourselves with prayer, meditation, enjoyable pursuits, and rest. Do not feel guilty when you choose to do so. Again, there is the caution that self-care can lead to self-absorption. However, someone who is mindful about his or her personal health, strength, and limitations is not to be viewed as necessarily self-absorbed. You are not any less of a Christian if you take care of yourself as you take care of others. Do not take on a life that completely drains you just because it is "expected." In other words, do not let others mold you according to *their* expectations. Do not fall into that trap.

Another aspect is *praying*. The church is full of people who serve God and others. Many are active in ministry and bring much help and teaching to others. It is common, however, that individuals who are involved in "prayer ministry" or "intercessory prayer" are seen as mystics or overly spiritual by many. To "hear from God" is often classified as weird. This is sad. Being in the ministry, I have heard several people say over the years that if their pastor or leaders are unavailable because they are off praying, then they are not really doing the work of the ministry. I have even heard people say that spending time in sincere prayer is "not doing enough for Jesus." Prayer is not a waste of time! No one can be effective without being in communication with God, our source of life! Again, Jesus Himself made sure He was in consistent fellowship with His Father through prayer.

Prayer is not a monologue. It is designed to be a dialogue. Most people are good at giving God a laundry list of requests. However, to hear from God is often overlooked. Many of the early "mystics" of the early church were ridiculed because of their relationship to God. Perhaps they really had something after all? Prayer warriors are not to be viewed as someone with an excuse to get out of serving in the breakfast fellowship. They are serving in an essential capacity. They may even be praying for you! If you love to pray and intercede for others, do not consider yourself a non-serving Christian. Do not allow someone else to define who you are or diminish your service unto God and others.

Many times, a person who *speaks up* is misunderstood. It is true that there are obnoxious and boisterous individuals who do indeed need to quiet down and back off. However, in my experience, I have come across more people who need to speak up and give voice to their thoughts and feelings.

Assertiveness is not a dirty word. Assertiveness is not the same as being obnoxious. Someone who is obnoxious and aggressive can be "in your face" about many things and difficult to be around. Assertiveness, very simply, is having the freedom to say how you feel and to ask what you need. A person can be soft-spoken and still be assertive and direct. I cannot tell you how often I come across men and women, especially women, who believe that being submissive means, to keep quiet. That is not submission –- that is being passive. To *demand* submission is oppressive.

One who speaks up is not necessarily being disrespectful or controlling. A person's voice is important. A wife or husband needs to feel like a part of the partnership called marriage. An employee needs to feel a part of the team and the process. Respect and a timely word can be critical in any relationship. If we believe we do not have a voice, we will not feel a part of the relationship, team, or process. Our voice is a large part of who we are. Without a voice, there is diminished understanding. If we are silenced, we feel less-than who we are.

One who is assertive is not the enemy either. Our society today has become overly sensitive, to the point where if any one speaks up, someone will feel offended. Often, the problem is with the receiver, not the transmitter! Parents are afraid to speak up to their children today because they do not want the children to hate them. Such parents are more interested in being friends to their child. The truth is, a child can always find a friend –- but they can't always find a good parent. Parenting is the second hardest job on earth (single-parenting is the hardest).

If children speak up, it doesn't necessarily mean they are disrespectful or disobedient. It is not best that "a child is best seen and not heard." That is a lie. Children can still be heard and feel like they are important, even though the parent has the last word. A parent can make the final decision, and children can still feel they were heard. If children are being mistreated, it is essential that they know they do have a voice. Their voice should not be oppressed, but encouraged.

Listening and speaking are critical aspects of good communication. If we are only speaking, we are missing out on very important perspectives. If we are only listening, we feel less-than capable of contributing to the relationship and process. Be careful not to misunderstand someone who speaks up as being pushy, critical, controlling, or self-centered. On the other hand, also be careful to not allow others to define you by their criticism just because you do speak up.

There is one final important piece to speaking up. We have this small, powerful word in the English language that has been seen as offensive in our current day and age. The word is "no". Parents, leaders, and Christians, who may use the word no for righteousness' sake, for protection, for discernment, for wisdom, etc., are often labeled as "intolerant" or "judgmental," among other names. Love does not mean that we tolerate everything. Understanding does not require us to tolerate everything. Intolerance has become more of a sin than sin itself.

There are quite a few things that are worthy of declaring no. Sin, certain lifestyles, arrogance, bad decisions, and mistreatment of individuals are a few of many. Speaking up accordingly may get a person in trouble and render a few names being placed upon them. It is true that no can be overly used, and as a result, frustration can set in. However, there are many non-negotiables that deserve the word no, such as affairs, drug abuse, crime, allowing certain behaviors in children or adults, unrighteous living, and many more. The problem is not saying no — the problem today is that we do not say *no* enough!

Another misinterpreted aspect is *forgiveness*. Today, even in the secular counseling world, forgiveness is a positive therapeutic approach. Many articles and books have been written about forgiveness. However, people who readily forgive others are often seen as weak, foolish, or with "no backbone." Instead, many view taking action against an offender or contemplating revenge as a more respectable option. After all, someone has to pay! Right?

Contemplating revenge can be very energizing indeed. The idea that we can concoct a very appropriate way to return the pain to the person or people who caused us pain is very attractive to us. I have spent hours with many couples and individuals in counseling who believe that if they could just return pain for pain to their offender, they would have justice and then feel so much better. After all, the Bible says, ". . . an eye for an eye and a tooth for a tooth. . . " (Ex. 21:24). However, Jesus changed that approach entirely — a very difficult thing to do.

In Matthew 5, Jesus spends much of the latter part of the chapter discussing aspects of personal relationships, a topic He covers quite often. He is teaching His disciples a different, more mature way of dealing with offenses and hurts. He raises the bar, in the name of personal freedom and maturity, by declaring the following:

You have heard that it was said, "An eye for an eye and a tooth for a tooth." But I say to you, do not resist him who is evil; but whoever slaps you on your right cheek, turn to him the other also. . . But I say to you, love your enemies, and pray for those who persecute you in order that you may be sons of your Father who is in heaven. . . For if you love those who love you, what reward have you? Do not even the tax-gatherers do the same? Therefore you are to be perfect, as your heavenly father is perfect (Matt. 5:38--48).

Can you imagine how strong a person needs to be in order to do as Jesus is asking? The Greek word for perfect here, *teleios*, means "of complete mental and moral character." To feel it is weak for someone to forgive goes against the true understanding of the concept of forgiveness. Someone with maturity and solid mental and moral character is stronger than anyone who desires revenge. However, the truth is that unforgiveness leads to resentment, then to bitterness, and then often to depression. Unforgiveness only hurts the one living in it.

A forgiving person is one who walks in freedom. Jesus made it very clear that if we do not forgive, we will not be forgiven (Matt. 6:14--15; Mark 11:26). In Matthew 18:21--35, Jesus teaches a parable about forgiveness and unforgiveness. One man was forgiven what amounted to 300,000 days of wages by his master, but was unwilling to forgive someone who owed him 100 days of wages. Jesus suggested that we are forgiven much, so we should forgive those who offend or "owe" us. Jesus said that for those who do not forgive, they are to be thrown into prison and turned over to the tormentors until they repay all their own offenses (Matt. 18:34). "He required that forgiveness be extended mercifully and repeatedly, and said that those who fail to forgive will only end up prisoners of their own condemning heart"

(Wardle 2001, 206). The prison and torment may not necessarily be a physical prison with torture. The prison and torture that we often find ourselves in when we do not forgive is that of anguish, resentment, and bitterness. When we forgive and release offenses, we are free from guilt and bitterness in our own lives. The torture of resentment and bitterness is eliminated through forgiveness. True freedom indeed!

Often, forgiveness is believed to be when we let someone "off the hook." Forgiveness is also seen as ultimately condoning their behavior. Both of these assessments are incorrect. Wardle provides an excellent understanding of forgiveness:

- Forgiving is not forgetting.
- Forgiving does not release the offender from responsibility.
- Forgiving does not mean the offended must be positioned to be re-injured.
- Forgiving is not pretending that it never happened.
- Forgiving does not mean it did not matter.
- Forgiving does mean that I release any desire for revenge, repayment, or punishment.
- Forgiving means that Christ will give me strength to live with the consequences of the offender's actions.
- Forgiving others flows from the forgiveness I have received in Christ.
- Forgiving means that I recognize my own weakness and sinfulness.
- Forgiving happens because of the blood of Christ, shed for me. (Wardle 2001, 207).

Someone who is able to forgive actually exhibits strong character and inner peace. Strength, and not weakness, is the character of one who forgives. Why is forgiveness so important? Because it is a part of who we are! It is a part of our identity in Christ. We are forgiven. Therefore, we can forgive. If we do not forgive, we are not forgiven. Ephesians 4:31–-32 clearly admonishes us: "Let all bitterness and wrath and anger and clamor and slander be put away from you, along with all malice. Be kind to one another, tender-hearted, forgiving each other, just as God in Christ also has forgiven you." Do not hold onto offenses –- they become the filters through which we understand others. Grudges become a part of who we are. So does forgiveness. Which one identifies you? By what name would you like to be known? Again, we can give only that which we have.

There are many other misunderstood people. Allow me to name a few more prominent ones:

A Quiet Person:

Misunderstood as having nothing to say.	**Truth:** May have lots to say, but is wise, slow to speak and slow to anger.
Misunderstood as being stupid.	**Truth:** May be intelligent on a different subject or matter altogether.
Misunderstood as unfriendly.	**Truth:** May be very loyal friend, but is careful with whom they associate.
Misunderstood as snooty or standoffish.	**Truth:** May be very humble and kind.
Misunderstood as afraid.	**Truth:** "Still waters run deep".

Isaiah 30:15 –- "In quietness and in confidence shall be your strength."(KJV)

Proverbs 17:27 –- "He who restrains his words has knowledge, and he who has a cool spirit is a man of understanding."

A Patient Person:

Misunderstood as apathetic.	**Truth:** Deliberate and careful.
Misunderstood as unmotivated.	**Truth:** Deeply self-motivated toward excellence and faithfulness.
Misunderstood as lazy.	**Truth:** Waiting for the right timing.
Misunderstood as "not having a clue".	**Truth:** Actually sees the big picture and considers many angles.

James 1:4 –– "But let patience have her perfect work, that ye may be perfect and entire, wanting nothing." (KJV).

A Person Who Cries:

Misunderstood as someone who is weak.	**Truth:** Someone who is strong and not afraid to show emotion.
Misunderstood as being too emotional.	**Truth:** Someone who is real. By the way: Crying is not an emotion; it is an expression of emotion. People cry when they laugh very hard. (People who show temper are emotional too!).
Misunderstood as attention-grabbing.	**Truth:** Someone who may need support and encouragement.

Psalm 120:1 –– "In my trouble I cried to the Lord, and He answered me."

A Person Who Is Gracious:

Misunderstood as a pushover.	**Truth:** Someone who cares and is not easily bent out of shape.
Misunderstood as tolerating sin.	**Truth:** He/she is humble and knows we all fall short; Take the log out of our own eye before we remove the speck from someone else's eye (Luke 6:41–42).
Misunderstood as not interested in truth.	**Truth:** Jesus was "full of *grace* and truth" (John 1:14, 17).
Misunderstood as too nice.	**Truth:** A person can be graciously assertive and kindly corrective. Admonishment is an important part of discipleship.

Proverbs 3:34 –- "He gives grace to the afflicted."

Romans 6:1-2 –- "Are we to continue is sin so that grace may increase? May it never be!"

Colossians 4:6 –- "Let your speech always be with grace, as though seasoned with salt."

Then there are judgments and labels made by simple observations with no basis for the opinions being made. For example, when a teenage girl is seen speaking to a boy in her class or in the school hallway, she may automatically be called a flirt. The girl may simply be friendly. I have known girls who were ridiculed by their circle of friends because they would peel away from the group to talk to a male classmate. Members of the group of her girlfriends would call her a flirt, among other names. There is a strong possibility the girl was mocked because someone else in her group had a crush on the guy and felt threatened. Being friendly does not necessarily constitute being flirtatious.

Another example is when someone is a good athlete. A good athlete may be labeled as prideful, stuck-up, or an egomaniac. While of course this could be true, much of the time confidence becomes equated with pride. A good athlete, or someone who is good at anything, needs to have a healthy level of confidence and self-awareness, without which they could not be successful.

Or if a student earns good grades, he or she is often called a "show-off." If co-workers approach their jobs with honesty, diligence, and integrity, they may be called "suck-ups" to their boss. Usually these types of names and labels are misunderstandings coming from individuals who are arrogant, immature, and envious. As a result, these assessments are not often accurate.

Avoiding the Dark Side

The *Star Wars* movies have been a cultural phenomenon for decades now. There is something about the high technology version of the fight between good and evil that attracts many people. The war between good and evil has been going on since the beginning of time and contains many stories of those who go from one kingdom to the other. When something good is used for evil, it becomes evil, misused, and misunderstood.

Dealing with spiritual gifts can be misunderstood as well. Not understanding the nature of the gift is one problem, and misusing the gift can be another issue altogether. Both will have the effect of feeling misunderstood, or misunderstanding God. Spiritual gifts are special attributes given by the Holy Spirit to every member of the body of Christ, according to God's grace, for the edification of the church, and for the glory of God. When we misuse spiritual gifts, or the glory is removed from God, we have crossed over to the dark side of feeding our own pride.

Spiritual gifts are not to be confused with the fruit of the Spirit (Gal. 5:22–23), which are attitudes and characteristics of anyone who has surrendered to Christ and follows Him. The fruit of the Spirit is what identifies a person as Christ-like. Also, spiritual gifts are not the same as natural talents, although they are often in concert with each other in an individual. Everyone, of every culture and of every religion has some type of natural talent. Spirit gifts are only for the believers in Christ, and can at times enhance the natural talents. Ultimately, though, even the natural talents come from God.

Add to the fact that each of us has a combination of temperaments, personality traits, and various levels of character traits that contribute to the use of the spiritual gifts. Temperament is the combination of inborn traits that subconsciously affect a person's behavior (LaHaye, 1991). Character is the real you, formed by a person's childhood environment, education, attitudes, basic belief system, principles, values, and motivations (LaHaye, 1991). Personality is the outward expression of who you are, which may or may not be an accurate presentation of our character, depending on how genuine we are (LaHaye, 1991). Considering how a person is wired, so to speak, can help us understand why certain gifts are used, or perhaps how certain gifts are misused or abused.

Below is a list of the spiritual gifts, indicated in the scriptures, as found in Romans 12, 1 Corinthians 12, and Ephesians 4. A general description of the gifts and their use are provided, as well as some ways that these gifts are misunderstood or misused. It is essential to know that these are gifts from God. He gives them to us to use, to be good stewards of the gifts. When we operate in these gifts on our own strength and power, we cross over to the dark side and the gifts no longer become gifts, but rather misused curses and self-centered expressions.

- **Administration** –- The ability to understand what makes an organization function, and the special ability to plan and execute procedures that accomplish the goals of the organization.
    - o **Dark side** –- being inflexible, uncooperative, and territorial in the administration of ideas and vision. Making a plan too personal and not in the interest of the greater good.
- **Apostleship** –- The ability to start and oversee the planting and development of new churches or ministries.
    - o **Dark side** –- Pride. The over-emphasis of the person's role over so many people.
- **Craftsmanship** –- The ability to creatively design and/or construct items to be used for the benefit of others.
    - o **Dark side** –- not staying according to plans. Making a project their creation for pride-feeding and not for the greater good.
- **Creative Communication** –- The ability to communicate God's truth through a variety of art forms.
    - o **Dark side** –- seeking the approval and applause of others, instead the doing for the glory of God. Becoming more performance-based in how one measures spirituality. Believing that the gift is exclusively yours.
- **Discernment** –- The ability to distinguish between truth and error; good and evil; and right and wrong; and to discern the spirits.
    - o **Dark side** –- overly judgmental, negative, and looking for demons behind every behavior or dysfunction.

- **Encouragement** -- the ability to present truth so as to strengthen, comfort, or urge to action those who are discouraged and wavering in their faith.
  - o **Dark side** -- doing it so much that one becomes insincere, coddling, or too tolerant of sin.
- **Evangelism** -- The ability to effectively communicate the gospel to unbelievers so they respond in faith and move toward discipleship.
  - o **Dark side** -- being overly dogmatic, unapproachable, too judgmental, or obnoxious.
- **Faith** -- the special ability to act on God's promises with confidence and unwavering belief in His ability to fulfill His promises.
  - o **Dark side** -- expressing faith so much that it becomes presumptuous, hopeful guess-work and dangerously misleading.
- **Giving** -- The ability to contribute money, time, and resources with cheerfulness, ease, and liberality, especially as it relates to the work of the Lord.
  - o **Darkside** -- Not exercising discernment to prevent being swindled. A giver is so willing to give, that any expressed need may look reasonable.
- **Healing** -- The ability to be God's means for restoring people to health and wholeness.
  - o **Darkside** -- For this person to suggest that when healing does not occur, it is because of lack of faith in the recipient. Also, this person can get so prideful that he or she believes healing is up to them, and lose sight of the true Healer.
- **Helps** -- The ability to attach spiritual and meaningful value to the accomplishment of practical and necessary tasks that free up, support, and meet the needs of others.

- o **Darkside** –- Similar to the one who gives –- has the potential of being taken advantage of by others; gets asked to help in everything and has a hard time placing boundaries and saying no, potentially leading to stress and resentment

- **Hospitality** –- The ability to care for people by providing fellowship, food, and shelter.
  - o **Darkside** –- Similar to the giver and helper. Can be taken advantage of. Often may put others ahead of their own family's well-being. For example, giving up a child's room for an outsider, with no end in sight.

- **Intercession** –- The ability to consistently pray on the behalf of and for others; thus seeing frequent and specific results.
  - o **Darkside** –- developing pride that they are the only ones that can pray for people, or that that their approach to prayer is the best way. Also, this sometimes can be seen as an "office" and can desire public acknowledgment. A true intercessor is a person who prefers to pray in private for others behind the scenes.

- **Interpretation** –- The ability to make known to the body of Christ the message of one who has spoken in tongues.
  - o **Darkside** –- often has been abused by people who simply want to have their voice known in the public arena, as if they are among the "few" who hear from God.

- **Leadership** –- The ability to cast vision, motivate, and direct people harmoniously to accomplish a common goal.
  - o **Darkside** –- Can become deaf to others' ideas and directions. Can become too bossy or controlling. Can ignore finer details of an operation causing financial and personal foolishness.

- **Mercy** –– The ability to cheerfully and practically help those who are suffering and who are in need.
    - o **Darkside** –– Similar to the helper and giver. Can find themselves being taken advantage of with no way out of the situation. May feel guilty when they feel they aren't doing enough. Has difficulty saying no.
- **Miracles** –– The ability to authenticate the ministry and message of God through signs, wonders, and supernatural interventions that glorify Him.
    - o **Darkside** –– They can feel as if they have a corner on the market of the supernatural. Pride takes over, to the point that they may even undermine the local pastor if the supernatural is not happening "enough."
- **Prophecy** –– The ability to reveal truth and proclaim it in a timely and relevant manner for understanding, correction, repentance, or edification.
    - o **Darkside** –– Can develop a condemning, negative spirit. Can believe they have the true pipeline to God and what He wants to say.
- **Shepherding** –– The ability to gather, nurture, care for, and guide people toward ongoing growth, especially as it relates to spiritual maturity and becoming like Christ.
    - o **Darkside** –– Similar to leadership. Can become unteachable –– after all he is "the man" or she is "the woman." Also, often experiences burnout, since too much is expected of them, either by others or self-imposed.
- **Teaching** –– The ability to understand, organize, clearly explain, and apply information, concepts, and truth to others; a good teacher helps others gain both knowledge and understanding.

- o **Darkside** –- can develop a "know-it-all" attitude. Gets "puffed up" and decreases in the motivation of love of impartation. Can become unteachable, since they have sat under "such great teachers."
- **Tongues** –- The ability to speak, worship, or pray in a language given by the Holy Spirit and unknown to the speaker. Most of the time it is for personal edification and spiritual warfare.
  - o **Darkside** –- Can present themselves as having a "special" relationship with God. That they are the only ones who can interpret what is being said. May tie this gift as evidence of a person's "true" salvation.
- **Wisdom** –- The ability to practically apply knowledge and truth effectively to meet a need in a specific situation.
  - o **Darkside** –- Will have difficulty admitting that others can be seen as a resource for an individual, since they have "far more" wisdom than anyone else. Can take rejection of their wisdom personally, instead of seeing it as rejection of the wisdom itself.

As you can see, much misunderstanding can occur with inaccurate labels and perceptions. We have to slow down in our assessments of others and situations. If we are too quick to render a judgment, then understanding is missed. Spiritual gifts are given by God to be used for the edification of the body of Christ and to positively influence the world. Misuse brings at least misunderstanding, and sometimes abuse and manipulation. However, anyone denying the importance of spiritual gifts for today does not understand the heart of God as giver. To believe that the gifts are no longer for today, frames God as a withholder of what we need. And to not use what God makes available to the believer is like being in the military without any weapons.

CHAPTER 8

Blueprint for Understanding

How blessed is the man who finds wisdom, and the man who gains understanding. For its profit is better than the profit of silver, and its gain than fine gold.

– Proverbs 3:13—-14

For this reason I also suffer these things, but I am not ashamed; for I know whom I have believed and I am convinced that He is able to guard what I have entrusted to Him until that day.

– 2 Timothy 1:12

Throughout the centuries, the biblical faith in God, as presented in the Old and New Testaments, was comprised of three components: information, inspiration, and revelation. All three are essential in understanding God, ourselves, and one another.

We have plenty of information about God, aspects that affect human development and psychological development. The Bible and the many resources that exist in print can be utilized to assist in the gaining of knowledge. As a nation and culture, we do very well with the information concept. The vast information highway of the computer Internet has dominated our senses with news, facts, and data at our fingertips. Church traditions throughout denominations have been strong in laying out information about their respective historical traditions and doctrines. To be "confirmed" as a Catholic or Lutheran, for example, several years of catechism are required to understand the doctrines and traditions of the specific church. Other traditions try to clearly teach the various doctrines and information needed for someone to understand their faith.

Other nations of the world have looked to America for the vast amounts of information and resources in many fields and professions. We were once the number one nation that produced missionaries in order to assist cultures with their needs and to teach and spread the gospel in their own respective communities. That has been changing.

Throughout history, there is an ebb and flow of truth and deception, peace and war, clarity and confusion, and happiness and sorrow. When the good times exist, we tend to take them for granted instead of realistically preparing for the difficult times that may lie ahead. Second Timothy 3:12--15 reminds us:

> And indeed, all who desire to live godly in Christ will be persecuted. But evil men and imposters will proceed from bad to worse, deceiving and being deceived. You, however, continue in the things you have learned and become convinced of, knowing from whom you have learned them; and from childhood you have known the scared writings which are able to give you the wisdom that leads to salvation through faith which is in Christ Jesus.

True wisdom and understanding are a result of knowing Jesus, surrendering to Him, and encountering Him. If we try to understand life without the wisdom of God's Word and Holy Spirit, we lessen the ability to make better decisions.

Fortunately, Joseph of the Old Testament was one who heard from God and discerned the times, and led the nation of Egypt to prepare for the coming famine. Genesis 41:1–49 tells the story. Joseph heard from God and understood the times. Joseph interpreted a dream that Pharaoh had and directed him to set aside one-fifth of all the grain and produce during seven years of plenty, in order to prepare for the coming seven years of famine. Pharaoh's response:

> Now the proposal seemed good to Pharaoh and to all his servants. Then Pharaoh said to his servants, "can we find a man like this, in whom is a divine spirit?" So Pharaoh said to Joseph, "Since God has informed you of all this, there is no one so discerning and wise as you are. You shall be over my house, and according to your command all my people shall do homage; only in the throne I will be greater than you." (Gen. 41:37--40)

Joseph's dependency upon God and awareness of the times provided an understanding of what he needed to do. He understood that preparation, even if it meant delayed gratification, would be essential for future survival. Even an idol worshiper such as Pharaoh understood that the wisdom of God would save his nation. If only our national leaders, church leaders, and families would do likewise.

Since understanding is essential for developing a lifestyle of good decision making, why is it that we are experiencing such bad decision-making skills that have less-than-expected outcomes? Why is it that there seem to be divisions in our families, churches, and political leadership? It is because of assumptions, agendas, pride, lies, dishonesty, woundedness, anger, rebellion, and wrong perceptions.

The proverb, "Never criticize a man until you've walked a mile in his moccasins" is usually credited to Native American sources, suggesting you can't really understand someone else unless you live their life, or walk in their shoes. As we have discussed, it is essential to consider many variables before we begin to understand God, ourselves, and other people. It requires effort, patience, seeking after truth, eliminating assumptions, good communication skills, and empathy. It begins with self-reflection.

I heard an old Native American story of an old Cherokee man teaching his grandson about life. "A fight is going on inside me," he said to the boy. "It is a terrible fight and it is between two wolves. One is evil –- he is anger, envy, sorrow, regret, greed, arrogance, self-pity, guilt, resentment, inferiority, lies, false pride, superiority, and ego. The other is good –- he is joy, peace, love, hope, serenity, humility, kindness, benevolence, empathy, generosity, truth, compassion, and faith. This same fight is going on inside you –- and inside every other person, too." The grandson thought about it for a minute and then asked his grandfather, "Which wolf will win?" The old Cherokee man simply replied, "The one you feed."

While we may be too busy to reflect on anything, it would behoove us to do so. We are moving or thinking too fast to stop, reflect, and consider. First we need to realize that God created us for relationship, and His intentions are good toward us. One of the common misunderstandings is that the Old Testament portrays a wrathful and judging God, while the New Testament paints a picture of a loving and gracious God. Perhaps this belief is behind the tendency in today's church to focus only on the New Testament for teaching.

First, I would like to summarize part one of this book, by providing some closing thoughts about God. Remember God has communicated and continues to communicate with us through content, tone of voice, and body language. His message is consistent through Old and New Testaments, albeit with varying emphasis. We have discussed several Bible anecdotes to frame the truth about God. Some others:

- God is love (1 John 4:7–9) –– He loves you.
- God is a giver (Gen. 1:29–30; and 2:18, 22; and 12:1–3; John 3:16) –– He desires to give to you.
- God is life (Gen. 2:7; John 14:6) –– He desires to give you new life.
- God is truth (Ps. 33:4; and 117:2; John 14:6; Heb. 6:18) –– He desires to reveal truth to you.
- God is just (Isa. 45:21) –– He will eventually make things right.
- God is holy and righteous (Lev. 11:44; 1 Pet. 1:16; Rev. 4:8) –– He gives His Holy Spirit and grace so that we can have the mind of Christ.
- God's *intent* is to see all saved (the choice is ours) (2 Pet. 3:9) –– He made provision for all people to be saved, and it is now *our choice* to accept His finished work.
- God is merciful and shows grace (Ps. 25:10) –– He cares for you.

After Adam and Eve took the fruit from the forbidden tree, they felt guilt and shame. God said to them earlier that if they took from the tree of the knowledge of good and evil, ". . . For in the day that you eat from it you shall surely die" (Gen. 2:17). The common use of the Hebrew and Greek words in scripture denote a natural, physical death (Orr, et al., 1986, 848). In the apostle Paul's writings, he speaks of natural death as well but will also allude to spiritual death. The overall connotation is the concept of "separation." When Adam and Eve sinned, they became separated from God –– they experienced spiritual death. Physical death would come eventually, and it too is a result of sin. The point is, even though they became separated from God and experienced it in their spirits, God did not reject them. Instead, He came to them to restore relationship! He continued to pursue them, despite their separation, which He does even today. Instead of keeping the separation in place, He came to Adam and Eve and continued in dialog and relationship.

However, God did something that was a shadow of things to come. "And the Lord God made garments of skin for Adam and his wife, and clothed them" (Gen.3:21). Essentially God had to kill an animal, to shed blood, in order to cover them with literal garments. Something else took the punishment for their sin, and blood was shed, in order for them to have their "shame" covered. God could have killed Adam and Eve, but His *grace* compelled Him to shed blood of an innocent substitute in order to save human kind. This act of grace was to be ultimately fulfilled centuries later through the blood of the One who was innocent and whose death was substitutionary in order to restore eternal relationship with God –– Jesus Christ! God's grace existed in the Old Testament, even in the midst of judgment against sin. We need to understand that God has judged sin. Yet, He will show grace, and we are spared of the sin judgment through Christ.

Other Old Testament accounts portray God as gracious and loving. Noah found favor in His sight (Gen. 6:8), and as a result, Noah and his entire family were spared the judgment of the world wide flood. Lot, despite his reluctance to leave the cities of Sodom and Gomorrah, was whisked away from the cities by the two angels, because the ". . . compassion of the Lord was upon him" (Gen. 19:16).

In 2 Chronicles 36:14--17, the compassion of the Lord was upon His people, even though it is clear that they continued to be unfaithful to God. At a point, though, as the people continued to mock God, God's word, and His servants, His compassion turned into judgment. Understanding God includes knowing His *first* response to all of us is to show compassion and grace. Then, when we respond, we experience God's favor. However, if we ignore and mock God's compassion and grace, judgment will eventually occur, and He would be justified to do so.

In the New Testament, the parable of the talents in Matthew 25:14--30 is a story that appears to have a harsh ending for one of the servants. Are we to understand Jesus as rendering such a harsh and final judgment upon someone simply because he or she buried a talent? The story provides an overlooked portioned that will help shed light on the issue.

Three men were given talents by their master who was about to go on a journey. The first man was given five talents, the second was given two talents, and the third was given one talent. The first two "immediately" (vs. 16--17) invested their talents, and both doubled what they were given. The third man "went away" and buried "his master's money" (v. 19). The master returned, after a long time away, and addressed each servant. As the first two reported their increase of the master's money, they were complimented by the master and given more responsibility and rewards -- "the joy of your master" (vs. 21--23).

The third addresses the master and makes a revealing statement:

> "Master, I knew you to be a hard man reaping where you
> did not sow, and gathering where you scattered no seed.
> And I was afraid, and went away and hid your talent in the
> ground; see, you have what is yours" (vs. 24--25).

Jesus called him a "wicked and lazy servant" (v. 26). The key to this entire story is the statement that the servant made –– "I knew you to be a hard man." This was his assumption and therefore his perception about his master. His actions conveyed his understanding of his master's intentions. Is this also our assumption about God? If so, we too will go away to hide and "bury" that which we have been given –– our gifts, talents, and even our life itself, all being gifts from the Master. If we understand God to be so hard, we will choose to run our own lives, rather than live in God's grace to please Him and experience blessings as a result. If, however, we understand God to be loving and gracious, we immediately desire to serve Him. We serve God *because* He loves us, not to gain His love. The result will be additional favor and blessings. If we see God as simply a "hard man" and reject and hide from Him, we truly do not understand God. To reject God based upon such an understanding will result in the condemnation for our lives as well.

When it comes to counseling, I find that it is often necessary to provide psychoeducation to the client about their condition and dysfunctions, as well as to their family members and loved ones. It can be quite helpful for someone to understand that their condition has consistent symptoms, outcomes, and reasons behind their thoughts, feelings, and behaviors. I do not express such knowledge as an excuse, but rather as an understanding of what it is that brings discomfort and broken relationships in a person's life.

It is also helpful to communicate hope, direction, and the potential for healing and change. It is amazing to me when I learn someone does not understand their condition and how it has affected their life. Shedding light on situations provides the understanding necessary for someone to begin to focus on what is needed to make changes in their life. A person's own "Ah-ha moment" if you will, can increase the potential for change.

Difficult situations, such as personality disorders, are a challenge to overcome, even with understanding, since brokenness and selfishness is burned onto someone's spirit. For example, Narcissistic, Borderline, and Histrionic personality disorders can be especially difficult to address because there is often denial, self-centeredness, deception, and bondage that exists in these disorders. The power of God as the change factor is often necessary, since simply understanding may not be enough to lead to change.

To improve our ability to understand ourselves and one another, we need to do the following, and we need the truth and transforming power of God's Spirit to help us:

- Not feel so easily or so quickly offended. Chances are the other person had no *intentions* of offending you. Give them some grace.

- Seek, ask, and explore reasons for another person's approach to life. Doing so means we become engaged and connected to others.

- Look at body language, and listen to tone of voice to gain a clearer understanding of what is being communicated. This requires less dependency on technology for communication and more effort to actually connect with people personally.

- Be forgiving and hold no grudges, because bitterness defiles many (Heb. 12:15). Remember, forgiveness sets *you* free as well.

- Be quick to discern and honor what we discern, in order to make better judgments about what we do with our life and who we allow into our life. Discerning benefits us. Morals, standards, and what we value are indeed important, especially if they are aligned with God.

- Be slow to judge but be wise in your judgments, taking the log out of your own eye first. Making judgments is necessary, but there is no condemnation in Christ Jesus, and only He has the final word over someone's life.

- Know that correction is essential for all of us, and it is not the same as criticism. Lawlessness and rebellion need to be addressed -- but with the righteousness of God.

- Earn the right to challenge and correct by being humble, patient, loving, and sincere.

- Be careful of labels on people, since they are usually related to outward appearances and past reputations. What you see is only part of the story and may not always even be true.

- Use your talents and gifts wisely, with care, with humility, and with gratitude for having them in the first place, for edification of others, not for personal gain. Gifts are given ultimately from God. We all have at least one gift -- no one is left bereft of being effective.

- Jesus is with you every step of the way. During times of pain and suffering He completely understands and is present for comfort, love, and peace. Perhaps, He may be calling you to be His arms of comfort and care for someone else? Your presence, not your explanation, may be all someone needs.

- Use Jesus as your model. He is loving, kind, patient, caring, attentive, seeking after truth, and confronting pride, fear, and rebellion when necessary, always looking to correct as to restore and redeem. When Jesus comes again, things will be justifiably different.

Today we need more inspiration and revelation. Good theology and doctrine are important, but the Western church has not done a good job of allowing for inspiration and revelation. The lack of a good, complete foundation leads to weakness and misunderstandings of God. On the other hand, if there is too much emphasis on experiential faith alone, the potential to be tossed around by many false doctrines increases. As a result, many believers have very little spiritual "substance" from which to draw upon in tough times. The doctrines have become watered down, perhaps even ignored, as it relates to suffering, waiting on God, and trusting Him no matter what.

How we worship, and perhaps the focus on our worship, has contributed to the present tendencies. Much of our music is loud, with light shows, and ultimately distracting. Once we are distracted, our focus on God is diminished. Our worship songs and choruses need to be foundational and revelatory. We need songs and lyrics that honor God and invoke trust in Him through questionable and difficult times. Our worship of God has become filled with feel-good songs giving us the impression that all we need is to feel good, in order to worship God.

While it is foundational to know that God loves us, delights in us, and has a plan for us, we also need to understand that God is still the object of our worship. It is important to include songs and hymns that declare God is good, in spite of our situation or circumstances, that He suffered for our transgressions and is risen, that by His stripes, death, and resurrection we can be healed, that He is Holy and praise worthy, and that His love for us never ends.

What we have is less and less substance and less about the character of God and more about us feeling better. As a result, many believers quickly bail out at the first sign of misunderstandings, offenses, and difficult times. The result has been that Christians have become "fair weather friends". When things become hard, we turn from God, since we have come to believe that He has to always explain Himself, or we are through with Him.

We all need a strong foundation of what it means to be a follower of Jesus. Understanding the foundation of faith ultimately will determine how we remain committed to truth. Can we confess as Peter did in John 6:68, when he did not know much at the time –- "Lord, to whom shall we go? [I understand that . . .] You have the words of eternal life. And we have believed and have come to know that You are the Holy One of God." We may not understand everything happening at the time, but can we remain faithful and committed to God, even in the midst of hurt, confusion, and disappointment?

We are all broken and need redemption and restoration in our life. Inspiration comes from knowing or observing someone's story as to how Jesus helped them overcome negative and hurtful areas of life, which can motivate us to do the same. Inspiration can shed light onto our own fears in order to understand our situations and life decisions better.

Revelation only comes from the Spirit of God. Revelation changes everything: assumptions, perceptions, intentions, decision-making approaches, healing of hurts, communication blockages, and even aspects of our life! Take the time to seek God, and ask Him for what you desire. Then wait and watch Him communicate to you. Be sure to be aware of His constant presence and His nature of giving and love. He will bring understanding to you, even if it is just by His presence alone.

Also, give yourself grace. If your broken heart and emotional pain have impeded the ability to see clearly and understand, seek Jesus and His Word for healing. Also, reach out to someone who you know cares, and allow his or her presence to be comforting to you. Isolating yourself is exactly what Satan wants. "Too many people suffer alone. And most people who suffer alone aren't looking for answers. Most people who suffer alone are looking for a friend –– a friend who understands" (Weece 2016, xv).

God sees you differently than you see yourself. The way we view our lives will impact the way we deal with others. Jesus desires us to love our neighbors as ourselves (Luke 10:27––28), but we need to know God's love for our lives first. I often say that it is more beneficial to operate from a standpoint of strength. And we can only give that which we have. We need to have Jesus strengthen our personhood.

As I said in my introduction, God understands us and the life we live on earth. He truly sees us accurately and in truth. He knows our inner desires and His plan for each individual. He knows our longing to be understood. We have been intricately created. The writer of Psalm 139:13––16 declares:

> For you formed my inward parts; You wove me in my mother's womb. I will give thanks to You, for I am fearfully and wonderfully made; wonderful are Your works, and my soul knows it very well. My frame was not hidden from You, when I was made in secret, and skillfully wrought in the depths of the earth; Your eyes have seen my unformed substance; and in Your book were all written the days that were ordained for me, when as yet there was not one of them.

We are going to sin –– to miss the mark –– the Bible makes that clear. But when we do, we may hear a couple of voices prompting our response. One voice could be the devil wanting to condemn us and suggest no hope. The voice we need to hear will be the Holy

Spirit's. He brings conviction for our transgressions, yet it is a hopeful conviction, one that leads to joyful repentance and not to despair. Discerning the difference is essential.

We have been given Jesus, and in our time of discouragement, we need to hear His voice above all others: "Neither do I condemn you." God did not send a theology to crush the lies of Satan—He sent Jesus! Weece says:

> He didn't send a bouquet of flowers and a greeting card. God sent His Son. He entered this world the way we entered this world – crying. And He left the world the way we'll leave the world – dying. But He didn't stay dead. And that's what separates Him from any other friend you have (Weece 2016, 8).

Understanding God, yourself, and others will bring peace to your life, even in the midst of storms and sufferings. God can provide the clarity we need, if we simply seek Him, and contemplate what truth is. May God supply you with His grace to understand that foundation—and when He does, rejoice!

Appendix

Disappointments with God –- Philip Yancey

Surprised by Suffering –- RC Sproul

The Problem of Pain –- C.S. Lewis.

Why Suffering? –- Ravi Zacharias

Doubt –- Os Guinness

Witness of the Stars –- E.W. Bullinger

God's Voice in the Stars: Zodiac Signs and Bible Truth –- Ken Fleming

When Skeptics Ask –- Norman L. Geisler

Evidence that Demands a Verdict –- Josh McDowell

Hearing God's Voice Above the Noise –- Stuart Briscoe

The Invisible War –- Donald Grey Barnhouse

Shaped by the Word –- M. Robert Mulholland, Jr.

Hard Sayings of the Old Testament –- Walter Kaiser, jr.

The Hard Sayings of Jesus –- F.F. Bruce

Encyclopedia of Bible Difficulties –- Gleason L. Archer, Jr.

The Bible Handbook of Difficult Verses –- Josh McDowell

The Knowledge of the Holy –- A.W. Tozer

When God Doesn't Make Sense –- Dr. James Dobson

Knowing God –- J.I. Packer

The Doubter's Guide to the Bible –- John Dickson

The Practice of the Presence of God –- Brother Lawrence

Happiness is a Choice –- Dr. Frank Minirth & Dr. Paul Meier

The Lies We Believe –- Chris Thurman

His Needs, Her Needs –- Willard F. Harley, Jr

References

http://biblehub.com/commentaries/pulpit/luke/24.htm. Pulpit Commentary, Electronic Data Base. 2010. Retrieved March 13, 2016.

http://news.yahoo.com/blogs/power-players/elton-john-george-w-bush-taught-lesson-040430553.html. July 25, 2012. By Jonathan Karl, Richard Coolidge, and Sherisse Pham. Retrieved April 7, 2014.

http://nypost.com/2016/03/17/my-husband-cheated-on-me-with-our-18-year-old-babysitter/Lindsey Putnam, reporter. Retrieved March 17, 2016.

http://www.pewinternet.org/fact-sheets/mobile-technology-fact-sheet/. Retrieved, June 21, 2015.

http://www.pewresearch.org/fact-tank/2014/12/22/14-striking-findings-from-2014/. Retrieved, May 4, 2016.

http://www.religionnews.com/2015/03/27/millennials-dont-judge-generation-sexual-morality-survey/ March 27, 2015. By Cathy Lynn Grossman. Retrieved April 6, 2015.

Belmonte, Kevin. (2011). *The Quotable Chesterton*. Thomas Nelson Publishers. Nashville, TN.

Boyd, Gregory A. (2004). *Repenting of Religion*. Baker Books. Grand Rapids, MI.

Bruce, F.F. (1983). *The Hard Sayings of Jesus*. InterVarsity Press. Downers Grove, IL.

Chapman, Gary. (2015). *The Five Love Languages*. Northfield Publishing. Chicago, IL.

Craig, Grace J. (1996). *Human Development*. Prentice Hall Publishers. Upper Saddle River, NJ.

Dickson, John. (2014). *A Doubter's Guide to the Bible*. Zondervan Publishing. Grand Rapids, MI.

Flynn, Leslie B. (1987). *Holy Contradictions*. Victor Books. Wheaton, IL.

Foster, Joshua D. and Ilan Shrira. 2009. "The Narcissus in All of Us: The Occupation with the Highest Suicide Rate." *Psychology Today*. http://www.psychologytoday.com/blog/the-narcissus-in-all-us/200908/the-occupation-the-highest-suicide-rate. Accessed February 3, 2016.

Frangipane, Francis. (2013). *Spiritual Discernment and the Mind of Christ*. Arrow Publications. Cedar Rapids, IA

Harrison, Everett F., Bromley, Geoffrey W., Henry, Carl F.H., Editors. (1982). *Baker's Dictionary of Theology*. Baker Book House. Grand Rapids, MI.

Hertel, P. (2004). Memory for emotional and non-emotional events in depression: A question of habit? In D. Reisberg and P. Hertel, (Eds.). *Memory and Emotion*. Oxford University Press. New York, NY. 186-216.

LaHaye, Tim. (1991). *Transforming Your Temperament*. Inspirational Press. New York, NY.

Leaf, Carolyn, M.D. (2009). *Who Switched off My Brain? Controlling Toxic Thoughts and Emotions*. Thomas Nelson Publishers. Nashville, TN.

Levine L.J. and Pizarro D.A. (2004). Emotion and memory research: A grumpy overview. *Social Cognition*, Vol. 22, No. 5, 2004, pp.530-554.

Lounsbrough, Craig D. (2015). *Assumptions, Agendas, and Danger.* Internet website article. Received November 1, 2015.

Mastering Life. (2008). *On Growing Up.* Mastering Life Ministries, Inc. January, Number 103.

Orr, James. Nuelsen, John L. Mullins, Edgar Y. Evans, Morris O. Kyle, Melvin Grove. (1986). *The International Standard Bible Encyclopedia.* Vol. II. William B. Eerdmans Publishing Co. Grand Rapids, MI.

Overman, Christian. (1996). *Assumptions That Affect Our Lives.* Micah 6:8 Publishers. Chatsworth, CA

Periodical Newsletter of the Voice of the Martyrs. Featured article, *Hunted Again.* April, 2016.

Ruiz, Don Miguel. (1997). *The Four Agreements: A Practical Guide to Personal Freedom.* Amber-Allen Publishing, Inc. San Rafael, CA.

Schacter, Daniel L., Gilbert, Daniel T., and Wegner, Daniel M. (2011). Semantic and episodic memory. *Psychology.* 2nd Edition. Worth, Inc. New York, NY. 240-241.

Terry, W. S. (2006). *Learning and Memory: Basic Principles, Processes, and Procedures.* Pearson Education, Inc. Boston, MA.

Turek, Frank. (2016). Six Reasons Why North Carolina Got it Right. *Tennessee Eagle Forum.* April 1, 2016. http://www.tneagleforum.org/.

Vine, W.E., Unger, Merrill F., White, William, Jr. (1985). *Complete Expository Dictionary of Old and New Testament Words.* Thomas Nelson Publishers. Nashville, TN.

Wardle, Terry. (2001). *Healing Care, Healing Prayer.* Leafwood Publishers. Abilene, TX.

Watkins, P.C.; Vache, K.; Vernay, S.P.; Muller, S.; Mathews, A (1996). Unconscious mood-congruent memory bias in depression. *Journal of Abnormal Psychology.* 105(1). 34–41.

Weece, Jon. (2016). *Me Too: Experiencing the God Who Understands.* Nelson Books. Nashville, TN.

Wright, Alan D. (2005). *Shame off You.* Multnomah Publishers. Sisters, OR.

About the Author

Christian counselor Dr. Robert B. Shaw Jr. is a Licensed Clinical Mental Health Counselor and Supervisor, dually licensed in Virginia and North Carolina. He is also an ordained minister, serving as a youth pastor, Christian education director, adult education director, musician, and executive pastor in churches in New Jersey, Colorado, Maryland, and in North Carolina, for over twenty-five years. He has also been a middle school and high school teacher and athletic coach in both the public and private school environments. Dr. Shaw has spent several years counseling in church settings and community agencies and counseling military personnel and their families near Ft. Bragg, North Carolina. He also ministers regularly in the Philippines. He specializes in trauma related issues; addictions; and victims of abuse, depression, anxiety disorders, life adjustment issues, loss and grief, counseling church leaders and pastors, adolescents, and adults. Dr. Shaw's is a unique prophetic voice in the kingdom caring for hurting people, and he serves as an adjunct professor for a Christian university, an author, and a sought-after conference speaker. Dr. Shaw has a Bachelor of Arts degree in religious studies from Wagner College, New York and a Master of Divinity degree from Christian

International Theological School, Florida. He also has a Master of Arts in professional counseling from Liberty University, Virginia and a Doctor of Ministry degree in formational counseling, a practical theology, from Ashland Theological Seminary, Ohio. He is a member of the American Association of Christian Counseling. Dr. Shaw enjoys running, sports, the beach, and spending time with friends and family.

Printed in the United States
by Baker & Taylor Publisher Services